NONVIOLENT STRUGGLE - The Foundation for Building Global Peace

Ven. Dr. Bhikṣuṇī Gioi Huong

Bao Anh Lac bookshelf 99

NONVIOLENT STRUGGLE
The Foundation for Building Global Peace

Presentation at the Humanitarian Affairs
Health Security and Global Peace Summit
August 26-31, 2024, Missouri, USA

Ven. Dr. Bhikṣuṇī Gioi Huong

TON GIAO Publishing

Contact:
HUONG SEN BUDDHIST TEMPLE
19865 Seaton Avenue, Perris, CA 92570, USA
Tel: 951-657-7272, Cell: 951-616-8620
Email: huongsentemple@gmail.com
thichnugioihuong@yahoo.com
https://www.facebook.com/Huong.Sen.Riverside
Web: www.huongsentemple.com

Cover image (from left to right, top to bottom):

1. Dr. Bhimrao Ramji Ambedkar (1891-1956) – Source: pngtree.com

2. Buddha and disciples - Source: phatgiao.org

3. Bodhisattva Thich Quang Duc (1897-1963) – Source: phatgiao.org

4. Mahatma Mohandas Karamchand Gandhi (1869- 1948) – Source: pngtree.com

5. King Ashoka (304-232 trước Công nguyên) – Source: pngtree.com

6. Pastor Martin Luther King, Jr. (1929-1968) – Source: pngtree.com

MỤC LỤC

CHAPTER 1

INTRODUCTION

1.1. REASONS FOR CHOOSING THE TOPIC OF NONVIOLENCE (AHIMSA): THE WORLD IN CRISIS OF WAR AND VIOLENCE (HIMSA)

The current global context in mid-2024 (twenty-first century) is unfolding in an extremely complex manner, with many instability, contradictions, grievances, hatred, and increasing disagreements. This has escalated armed wars, and violent massacres (himsa), with serious escalations like the Russia-Ukraine conflict, Israel-Hamas, and the civil war in Yemen involving the Houthis, Myanmar, Pakistan, Afghanistan, Syria, and many other places.

Lack of love, compassion, respect, and generosity leads to "the stacked fire of conflict and hatred" potentially spreading across entire regions. The world order is in jeopardy, with many painful consequences including a high number of innocent civilian casualties. According to Al Jazeera,[1] in the Hamas-Israel conflict alone, there were at least 36,224 fatalities, including over 15,000 children, and more than 81,777 injuries.

1 Al Jazeera, (2024), Israel-Gaza war in maps and charts: Live tracker. https://www.aljazeera.com/news/longform/2023/10/9/israel-hamas-war-in-maps-and-charts-live-tracker

The United Nations and many countries worldwide are calling for an end to conflicts, promoting humanitarian efforts, peace solutions, and ceasefires, yet effectiveness has been limited.

Nonviolence is the building block

Peace for us and the world. (Image: Master Thich Nhat Hanh)

1.2. NONVIOLENCE IS THE KEY TO RESOLVING THE CRISIS OF VIOLENCE

The term "nonviolence" (ahimsa) signifies the virtue of "non-harming," advocating for the non-use of physical force and instead employing methods of peaceful negotiation (ahimsa) or gentle acts of compassion when interacting with all individuals, living beings, groups, communities, or nations worldwide. This is one of the prominent virtues in Indian religions such as Buddhism, Jainism, Hinduism, and in the modern era of the twentieth century, many political figures have also embraced this spirit of nonviolence in their struggles for independence or against social injustices, such as Mahatma Gandhi (1869-1948), Dr. Bhimrao Ramji Ambedkar (1891-1956), Bodhisattva Thich Quang Duc (1897-1963), Martin Luther King Jr. (1929-1968)

In this article, I propose to discuss the teachings of the Buddha on nurturing the spirit of nonviolence and non-harming (ahimsa) based on compassion and wisdom. Additionally, I will explore the application of this nonviolent struggle spirit by King Aśoka (ancient times) and modern saints like Mahatma Gandhi, Dr. Bhimrao Ramji Ambedkar, Bodhisattva Thich Quang Duc, Martin Luther King Jr. in their effective efforts through dialogue and action to end conflicts, social injustices, religious oppression, and to restore peace to the community at large.

What did the Buddha think about war crisis? (Image: Internet)

CHAPTER 2

AHIMSA IN BUDDHISM

2.1. DEFINITION

Ahimsa (Hindi: अहिंसा, Sanskrit: ahiṃsā): The prefix "a" is negation, "hiṃ: means desire, "sā: means to kill. Therefore, ahiṃsā means non-desire to kill (non-harming), nonviolence. In contrast, hiṃsā (without the prefix a) means harm, violence.

In Buddhism, Jainism, and Hinduism, ahimsa is a way of life, a spirit, a principle of living that is completely harmless, not only to oneself and others but also to all beings and all things. Therefore, because of ahimsa, Buddhists vow to be vegetarians (avoiding eating the flesh of animals), take refuge in plants, protect the environment, and do not harm the surrounding nature.

Nonviolence in Buddhism stems from the virtues of compassion and letting go, which lead beings away from suffering and ignorance, guiding them towards liberation and Nirvana. Therefore, Buddhism advocates for universal, boundless love. Even if one has to endure hardship, mistreatment, and attacks, one should still maintain love for all beings, including enemies and those opposed to oneself, as Buddha taught: "Compassion brings all beings peace, both spiritually and materially."[2]

Ahimsa does not mean being timid, passive, or afraid to wield weapons. On the contrary, it is very proactive, embodying a spirit of courage and steadfastness, firmly adhering to the principle of love, persistently and resolutely convincing others, acting and sacrificing through nonviolent methods that do not harm the target, avoiding bloodshed, killing, and elimination, all because of our boundless love for them.

In religion, the meaning of ahimsa is detailed and profound. It signifies non-harm, non-killing, and not injuring or violating others or living beings through body (physical harm), speech (bullying, abusive language, words like knives and hammers that drive people to suicide), and harmful intentions (wishing to harm others), causing suffering to people and animals. This is also the first precept in the Five Precepts of Buddhists,[3] the first precept [4]in the Bodhisattva Precepts for both lay and monastic practitioners[5], and the second pārājika (defeat) rule for Bhikkhus[6] and Bhikkhunis[7] in the Vinaya.

---

2 The Great Treasure Sūtra (Kinh Đại Bảo Tích)
https://phatphapungdung.com/phap-bao/kinh-dai-bao-tich-123383.html

3 Five precepts of lay Buddhists:

1) Avoid killing and harming
2) Avoid theft
3) Avoid lying
4) Avoid sexual immorality
5) Avoid drinking alcohol

https://thuvienhoasen.org/images/file/oFn2tZ1G0QgQADZD/quyytambaovanamgioi.pdf

4 The Lay Bodhisattva Precepts: there are 6 main precepts and 28 minor precepts.
https://giacngo.vn/gioi-bo-tat-tai-gia-post15448.html

5 The monastic Bodhisattva precepts: there are ten major precepts and forty-eight minor precepts.
https://www.daotranglienhoa.com/wp-content/uploads/2023/08/kinh_pham_vong.pdf

6 The Four Pārājikas Precepts of the Bhikkhu.
https://en.dhammadana.org/sangha/vinaya/227.htm

7 The Eight Pārājikas Precepts of the Bhikkhuni.
https://www.accesstoinsight.org/tipitaka/vin/sv/bhikkhuni-pati.html

This demonstrates that ahimsa is the foremost and most crucial principle in Buddhism, guiding the behavior, speech, and attitudes of both lay and monastic disciples towards nonviolence. The principle applies not only to humans and large animals but also to insects, plants, and even tiny bacteria. Buddhists believe that not harming others is one of the most important ways to reduce suffering, which is the central goal and primary precept of Buddhism.

Therefore, in the Encyclopaedia Britannica, ahimsa[8] is defined in the context of Indian religions such as Jainism, Hinduism, and Buddhism as the ethical principle of not causing harm to other living beings.

Similarly, Wikipedia defines ahimsa[9] as the ancient Indian principle of nonviolence applied to all living beings. It is a key virtue in Indian religions such as Jainism, Buddhism, Hinduism, and Sikhism. It is the first vow in Jainism (Pancha Mahavrata).[10]

https://hoavouu.com/a9143/ii-tam-phap-ba-la-di

8 Ahimsa in Encyclopaedia Britannica https://www.britannica.com/topic/ahimsa

9 Ahimsa in Wikipedia https://en.wikipedia.org/wiki/Ahimsa

10 Five Vratas of Jainism:

1) Ahimsa, which means non-harm

2.2. AHIMSA AS THE PRECEPT OF AVOIDING KILLING

Precepts (sila) mean morality. Vinaya is discipline, the daily observances, and the rules and regulations that must be adhered to.

Precepts and discipline are very important in the practice of Buddhism and embody the spirit of nonviolence towards all beings. The precepts help Buddhist disciples prevent evil and crude violence (himsa) in body, speech, and mind, and help cultivate goodness (ahimsa). The Buddha established the precepts for both lay and monastic disciples to uphold in their daily lives. This is part of the threefold training (Threefold Learning: Sila-Samadhi-Panna) aimed at eliminating defilements and ignorance, leading to liberation and enlightenment.

Buddha advised Angulimala to put down the inner and outer sword. (Image: Giác Ngộ Online)

---

2) Satya, which means not talking to each other

3) Asteya, i.e. non-stealing

4) Brahmacharya, which means not committing adultery

5) Aparigraha, which means freedom from earthly bondage

https://jainworld.jainworld.com/phil/pmvratas.htm

To purify the body and mind and promote a peaceful and harmonious society, the Buddha established many precepts such as the Five Precepts, the Ten Precepts, the 250 Precepts, and the 348 Precepts. Among these, the Five Precepts (not killing, not stealing or infringing on others' property, not lying to harm others, not engaging in sexual misconduct, and not consuming alcohol or intoxicants) are the fundamental rules guiding human behavior towards goodness. Of these, the precept of not killing (ahimsa) is the most important.

In Buddhism, there are seven categories of disciples: monks (bhikkhus), nuns (bhikkhunis), female probationers (sikkhamanas), male novices (samaneras), female novices (samaneris), laymen (upasakas), and laywomen (upasikas). The first requirement for all of them is to observe the precept of ahimsa, abstaining from killing (himsa). Therefore, throughout Buddhist history, we have never seen wars involving bloodshed or inflicting injuries on others.

Abstaining from killing (himsa) means not only refraining from killing humans and animals but also respecting the life of plants. Thus, according to one precept, monks and nuns are not allowed to cut down trees or relieve themselves on grass or into rivers and streams, except under special circumstances.

Both lay and monastic disciples vow not to take any life, from humans and animals to nature. They must not kill or ask others to kill, as such acts of violence will lead them to hell. Conversely, releasing lives and practicing non-harming (ahimsa) will lead to rebirth in the heavenly realms and human world, as taught in the Anguttara Nikaya:

"O Bhikkhus, whoever fulfills the three factors of killing will fall into hell. What are the three? Killing themselves, encouraging others to kill, and rejoicing in killing. Whoever fulfills these three factors, O Bhikkhus, will fall into hell.

"O Bhikkhus, whoever fulfills the three factors of abandoning killing will be reborn in the heavenly realms. What are the three?

Abandoning killing themselves, encouraging others to abandon killing, and rejoicing in the abandonment of killing. Whoever fulfills these three factors, O Bhikkhus, will be reborn in the heavenly realms."[11]

Nonviolence and avoiding harm to people and animals are fundamental principles taught by the Buddha, Shakyamuni. This is emphasized in many scriptures, such as in the following verse:

He abused me, he struck me,
he overpowered me, he robbed me.
Those who harbor such thoughts
Will never be free from hatred.
He abused me, he struck me,
he overpowered me, he robbed me.
Those who do not harbor such thoughts
Will be free from hatred.
(Dhammapada, Chapter 1, Verses 3 and 4)[12]

Therefore, in Buddhism and Buddhist countries, governments are encouraged to implement the highest penalty (ahimsa) as life imprisonment, granting the offender the chance to reform and change their mindset, instead of imposing the death penalty (himsa). As the Buddha once advised a king in the past:

"Great King, you might think that you can eradicate all crimes by killing criminals, imprisoning them, fining them, reprimanding them, or exiling them. But this will never be completely successful: there will always be survivors who will

11 Anguttara Nikāya (Tăng Chi Bộ). Chapter III – Three Dharmas. XI. The Enlightenment. Translated by the Most Ven. Thích Minh Châu. https://www.budsas.org/uni/u-kinh-tangchibo/tangchi03-1116.htm

12 Dhammapada. Chapter Twin Verses. The 3rd and 4rd verses. Trans by Thích Minh Châu https://phatphapungdung.com/kinh-phap-cu-pham-song-yeu-cau-4-201977.html

continue to trouble your kingdom and oppose you. Great King, use methods of non-harm (ahimsa)."[13]

Why does the Buddha advise against killing?

Violence and killing not only harm others and disrupt the community but also create bad karma for the perpetrator, leading to inner turmoil and negative consequences in this life. Therefore, avoiding violent actions is the first step in the Buddhist system of training in ethics, meditation, and wisdom (sila-samadhi-panna).

Due to anger, using violent weapons (himsa) take human life. (Image: Internet)

2.3. AHIMSA AS THE ABOLITION OF CAPITAL PUNISHMENT

Capital Punishment: Capital means death, and punishment refers to a penalty. The highest penalty under the law is to sentence a criminal to death by means such as shooting, lethal injection, hanging, stoning, or burying alive until death. This is a special punishment applied to those who commit severe crimes,

13 Dìgha Nikàya (Trường Bộ kinh) I, Kūṭadanta Sutta, p.135 English tran. by Pali Text Society.
https://thuvienphatviet.com/thich-tue-sy-thich-nguyen-giac-dich-nen-tang-kinh-te-hoc-tu-cai-nhin-phat-giao/

lose their humanity, or engage in unethical behaviors (such as murder, drug trafficking, rape, political crimes) that need to be removed from society and serve as a deterrent to others. The criminal codes of different countries may prescribe either the death penalty or life imprisonment.

Capital punishment symbolizes violent punishment under the pretext of "administering justice" and "an eye for an eye," resembling revenge. However, this contradicts the Buddhist precept against killing, the virtue of respect for life, compassion, altruism, morality, and the principle of nonviolence (ahimsa).

Human life is very precious. According to Buddhist teachings, it is exceedingly difficult to be born as a human, likened to a blind turtle rising to the surface of the water once every hundred years to find a floating tree trunk. Each century, the blind turtle surfaces, while the tree trunk drifts east and west with the wind, making it nearly impossible for the turtle to catch the trunk. Similarly, being born as a human is a rare and precious opportunity.

People protest to abolish the death penalty. (Image: Internet)

There is a proverb: "To err is human." Even for those who commit serious crimes, it is better to give them an opportunity to repent and turn their lives around by serving the community. This approach is more beneficial than violent execution.

Buddhism believes in the law of cause and effect (karma) and emphasizes actions based on the Four Right Efforts (Catvari Prahanani):[14]

The Four Right Efforts (Catvari Prahanani) in Buddhism can be summarized as follows:

Diligence in preventing unwholesome states that have not yet arisen:

Making an effort to prevent negative or harmful thoughts, actions, and behaviors from arising.

Diligence in abandoning unwholesome states that have already arisen:

Making an effort to eliminate negative or harmful thoughts, actions, and behaviors that have already arisen.

Diligence in developing wholesome states that have not yet arisen:

Making an effort to cultivate and bring forth positive and beneficial thoughts, actions, and behaviors that have not yet arisen.

Diligence in maintaining and perfecting wholesome states that have already arisen:

Making an effort to sustain, develop, and perfect positive and beneficial thoughts, actions, and behaviors that have already arisen.

By adhering to these principles, individuals can lead a life of moral integrity and contribute to a peaceful and compassionate society.

If we treat prisoners violently, we will also face the

14 The Four Right Efforts or the Four Right Dharmas (Catvari Prahanani) https://phatgiao.org.vn/tu-dien-phat-hoc-online/ba-muoi-bay-pham-tro-dao-k27067.html#google_vignette

consequences. The principle of karma is regarded as a moral standard for Buddhists. Good will be protected, and evil will be prevented if everyone internalizes the concept of karma as taught by the Buddha.

One might escape worldly laws or deceive their own conscience, but one cannot escape the law of karma. Thus, "Bodhisattvas fear the cause, sentient beings fear the effect." This means that a wise person, who understands karma deeply, will fear committing bad deeds, whereas those who do not understand the law of karma will only fear the punishment that results from their actions.

Nevertheless, fearing both the cause and the effect is better than not fearing anything at all.

There is a story about a king who fell into hell for sentencing a criminal (a thief) to death, as recounted in the Cakkavatti Sīhanāda Sutta:

In the story of the Temiya Jataka, the Buddha was born as a crown prince. He was brought to his father, the king, while the king was in the judge's seat, sentencing criminals to death. It cannot be said that this sentencing was wrong; the king was merely fulfilling his duties.

However, the future Buddha (the crown prince) remembered that in a past life, he had also been a king who sentenced people to death. As a result, he had suffered in hell for eighty thousand years.

The story[15] goes as follows:

> "The wet nurse brought Prince Temiya to serve his father, King Bàrànasì, who loved him dearly. At that time, soldiers brought in four criminals for the king to judge. Depending on the

15 Ten Paramitas. Temiya Jàtaka. The Story of Temiya Bodhisatta practices: the Paramitas of Renunciation. Bhikkhu Hộ Tông (Vansarakkhita Maha Thera) https://www.budsas.org/uni/u-thapdo/thapdo-03.htm

severity of their crimes, the king sentenced the four criminals to either death or imprisonment. Upon hearing his father's judgments, Prince Temiya was greatly horrified by the punishments. He then reflected, 'From where have I been born into this life?' Thanks to his intuition, he recalled his past lives He further thought, "Where was I before ascending to the Tavatimsa Heaven?" He realized that he had come from the boiling cauldrons of hell. Before falling into hell, he had been an emperor in the capital of Bàrànasì.

He then thought, "In the future, when I grow up, I will inherit the throne from my father. I will have to judge and sentence criminals (to execution or imprisonment in chains), and thus I will inevitably fall into hell as I did in my past life."

Realizing this, he became disillusioned and deeply fearful of the royal duties and the consequences that come with them. This insight made him renounce the idea of kingship and develop a profound aversion to the violent actions associated with ruling as a king (Jàtisasarannàna). He remembered that he had descended from the Tavatimsa Heaven."

Death penalty, taking a life. Is that justice? (Image: Internet)

From that moment, the Bodhisattva Prince Temiya (who would later become Buddha Shakyamuni) practiced the virtue of renunciation, avoiding actions that create bad karma (himsa) for all beings, even criminals. Buddhism perceives that all people are fundamentally good, and the main purpose of Buddhism is to educate, transform, and reform rather than destroy. If someone is sick, Buddhism strives to cure the person of the illness rather than destroy the person carrying the disease. Buddhism views criminals as individuals with mental issues combined with ignorance (avijja).

Buddhism believes that all people are fundamentally good, and its main goal is to educate, transform, and reform rather than destroy. If someone is sick, Buddhism strives to cure the person of the illness rather than destroy the person carrying the disease. If someone commits a serious crime, Buddhism views the criminal as someone with mental issues combined with ignorance.

Thus, the primary goal of Buddhism is to eliminate the root cause of ignorance rather than to eliminate the ignorant person. This can be achieved through education, compassion, and nonviolence (ahimsa). By addressing the root causes of harmful behavior, Buddhism aims to cultivate understanding, wisdom, and compassion in all individuals, promoting a peaceful and harmonious society.

Through this approach, Buddhism aims to cultivate understanding, wisdom, and compassion in all individuals, thereby promoting a peaceful and harmonious society. By addressing the root causes of harmful behavior, Buddhism seeks to educate and transform individuals, helping them to realize the true nature of their actions and their consequences.

In Buddhism, there is a saying: "Even building nine tiers of a pagoda is not as good as saving one person."

In summary, based on the fundamental teachings of the Buddha from Buddhist scriptures and the compassionate and wise perspectives of Buddhist kings in ancient Asian history, as mentioned above, we wholeheartedly support the call to world leaders in countries that practice capital punishment to abolish this penalty in the spirit of boundless compassion of Buddhism.[16]

2.4. AHIMSA IS AN EXPRESSION OF COMPASSION

Ahimsa is an expression of compassion. By cultivating compassion, one refrains from nurturing violent, harmful tendencies that cause physical and mental harm to others. The Buddha regarded all beings as his own children, and therefore he advised his disciples to refrain from killing or harming any living beings under any circumstances. On the contrary, one should honor the sacred value and protect the lives of all beings.

People and animals both have equal Buddha nature and love each other. (Image: Giác Ngộ Online)

16 For full information, please read the second appendix at the end of this book: *The Fundamental Teachings of the Buddha on the Death Penalty*. Ven. Dr. Bhikṣuṇī TN Gioi Huong.

When the Buddha was alive, he condemned the sacrificial rituals of the Brahmins (who killed dozens, and hundreds of goats, sheep, and cows to offer to the gods) and criticized the hunting pleasures of kings and commoners. Protecting, respecting, and elevating the value of life is a central concept of Buddhist ethics. This principle is exemplified in the Metta Sutta (Loving-kindness Discourse):[17]

May everyone and all species live in safety and happiness, with gentle and carefree thoughts.

May all creatures on earth live peacefully, the weak, the strong, the tall, the short, the big, the small, the ones we can see, the species that we cannot see, species that are near, species that are far away, species that have been born and species that are about to be born.

Pray that no one will kill any other, no one should take anyone's life lightly, no one out of anger or malice will wish for anyone to suffer and be miserable.

Like a mother protecting her only child with her life, let us treat all living things with compassion.

Let us bring our unlimited compassion to cover the whole world and all living things, from top to bottom, from left to right, our compassion is not separated by anything, our mind is no longer lingering on one thing. some resentment or hatred. At any time, when walking, standing, sitting, lying down, as long as we are awake, we vow to maintain compassion and mindfulness within ourselves. A compassionate lifestyle is the most beautiful lifestyle.

Not straying into wrong views, gradually eliminating desires, living a healthy lifestyle and achieving enlightenment, the practitioner will definitely escape birth and death.

17 Metta Sutta. Discourse on Loving-kindness. https://www.huongsentemple.com/index.php/vn/phat-phap/kinh-ta-ng-ca-a-cha-a-hs/6256-nghi-le-hang-ngay-20

Compassion is the most beautiful state of mind in this world and is synonymous with non-harming (ahimsa). The Buddha advised his disciples to frequently meditate on the Four Immeasurables (loving-kindness, compassion, sympathetic joy, and equanimity), extending boundless love to all sentient beings, whether known or unknown, in all ten directions (east, west, south, north; southeast, southwest, northeast, northwest; above and below).

Because of the psychological principle that "everyone fears the sword and everyone fears death," one should empathize with others by considering one's own feelings, and thus, refrain from killing or inciting others to kill. Furthermore, the Buddha taught that although beings are subject to different karmic retributions, they share the same inherent nature. Animals, like humans, experience hunger, thirst, and suffering, and seek comfort and security. Therefore, killing any creature, from a chicken, duck, pig, or goat, to even an insect like an ant or a worm, is an act of harming Buddha-nature and taking a life. Hence, the Buddha taught:

Hatred is, indeed, never appeased by hatred in this world.
It is appeased only by loving-kindness.
This is an ancient law.

People, other than the wise, do not realize,
"We in this world must all die,
(and, not realizing it, continue their quarrels).
The wise realize it and thereby their quarrels cease.
(Dhammapada, Chapter 2, Verses 5 and 6).[18]

When we kill a person or an animal, their resentment and hatred overflow and are difficult to extinguish. Because they

18 Dhammapada, Chapter 2, Verses 5 and 6. Vietnamese trans. By Thich Minh Chau https://www.nguyenthuychonnhu.net/index.php/bdt/1355-1-lgtkpc-2-dt

were killed by us for their position, for their weakness, they will harbor hatred and wait for an opportunity to retaliate. Therefore, do not sow such intense enmity for a delicious morsel, do not sow enmity for the pleasure of hunting. On the contrary, we should practice releasing life, performing acts of charity, and thereby extinguishing enmity. Therefore, compassion, nonviolence, and tolerance provide us with the spiritual strength to resist any motivations leading to wrongful actions.

In the book *The Buddha's Teaching on Love* by Master Thich Nhat Hanh, it is recounted that[19] one day, several monks came to report to the Buddha that the forest where they resided was troubled by malevolent forces. They asked the Buddha how to bring peace to the forest. The Buddha taught them that the beings in that forest were suffering, causing their own suffering, and in turn, causing suffering to others. Therefore, the monks should practice the meditation of loving-kindness (Metta Sutta). By practicing Loving-kindness meditation, the energy of loving-kindness and compassion would permeate through them and extend to all beings in the forest.

Encouraged by this teaching, the monks recited and practiced the Metta Sutta. Several months later, the forest became peaceful. The energy of Loving-kindness within the monks had permeated through them, enabling them to accept and understand the suffering of the beings in the forest. These beings, having heard the Metta Sutta, also began to practice it. Thus, the forest became serene and happy, thanks to the presence and practice of loving-kindness meditation by the monks.

This case demonstrates how the Metta Sutta can transform both individuals and environments. Practicing loving-kindness meditation brings ease, comfort, and happiness to one's mind and surroundings, making them peaceful and joyful.

---

19 Master Thich Nhat Hanh. *The Buddha's Teaching on Love.* https://langmai.org/tang-kinh-cac/vien-sach/thien-tap/thuong-yeu-theo-phuong-phap-but-day/chuong-ii-bai-thuc-tap-thu-nhat/nang-luong-tu-bi/

2.5. AHIMSA AS LIBERATION AND COMPASSIONATE SAVING OF LIVES

Human life or the lives of animals are very precious, because of the Buddha's equal nature among all beings as the Buddha often teaches: "The Buddha's sentient beings are often silent. I am the Buddha who has become, sentient beings are the Buddha who will become" or "Equal Enlightenment pervades all sentient beings."[20]

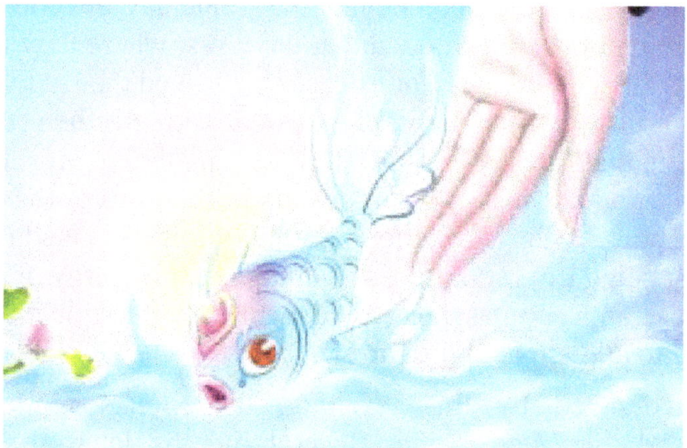

Fish are happy to return to their home ocean.

(Image: Internet)

The Brahmajàla Sūtra [21]teaches that: Buddhists regard all beings in the six realms as their parents from many lifetimes. If

20 The Buddha's Teaching of the Mahayana Infinite Life Dignified Pure Equality Enlightenment Sūtra (Phật Thuyết Đại Thừa Vô Lượng Thọ Trang Nghiêm Thanh Tịnh Bình Đẳng Giác Kinh).Chinese translated by Hạ Liên Cư (hội tập). Vietnamese trans. by Thích Đức Niệm & Minh Chánh. Tôn Giáo Publishing. Hà Nội. 2009.
https://ph.tinhtong.vn/Home/Doc/phuc-giang-kinh-vo-luong-tho-lan-2-co-luu-to-van-000037?t=4

21 Brahmajāla Sutta: The All-embracing Net of Views. Translated from the Pali by

one sees someone about to kill an animal, one should find a way to rescue it, so that they are liberated from suffering, and return to their natural environment. The Mahàprajnàparamitàsastra[22] states: "Among all virtues, saving lives is the greatest virtue."

Saving lives and liberating beings must stem from compassion and should be practiced at all times. For example, if encountering a robber intending to kill, one should seek to rescue; report to authorities upon seeing individuals abducted for organ trafficking; release a branch to help a group of ants or dogs swept away by water; on the road, stop the vehicle to allow deer, chickens, ducks, pigs, and cows to pass safely, and so on.

Saving lives and liberating beings, rooted in compassion, aims to bestow life upon humans and all creatures facing imminent death. Thus, saving lives and liberating beings should promptly deliver humans, captives (abducted individuals), and animals from death and return them to their natural habitat safely, without being concerned about formalities.

Saving lives and liberating beings is a deed that every person should do with a compassionate heart, especially refraining from actions that harm life and injure animals.

Bhikkhu Bodhi. 2010. Alternate translation: Thanissaro
https://www.accesstoinsight.org/tipitaka/dn/dn.01.0.bodh.html
https://www.daotranglienhoa.com/wp-content/uploads/2023/08/kinh_pham_vong.pdf

22 Mahàprajnàparamitàsatra (Luận Đại Trí Độ). Nàgàrjuna (Long Thọ). Trans from Sanskrit to Chinese: Kumārajīva. Trans from Chinese into Vietnamese: Thích Thiện Siêu. Published by Buddhist Studies in Vietnam Research Institute. 1997.
Awakening of Faith in the Mahāyāna is an influential Mahayana Buddhist treatise for East Asian Buddhism. Though traditionally attributed to the second century CE Indian master Aśvaghoṣa, no Sanskrit version is extant and it is widely regarded by many contemporary scholars as having been composed in China.
https://en.wikipedia.org/wiki/Awakening_of_Faith_in_the_Mahayana
https://phatphapungdung.com/phap-bao/luan-dai-tri-do-70088.html

2.6. AHIMSA IN VEGETARIANISM

Vegetarianism is a method to nurture ahimsa, the principle of nonviolence, especially towards animals. Everyone possesses some degree of compassion, caring for humans, animals, fellow beings, and the environments they live in. We do not wish to harm or infringe upon the lives of animals, so many people undertake vegetarianism, observing the precepts of the Buddhist household.

Pure vegetarian dishes are nutritious and do not violate animals. (Image: Internet)

The United States has estimated[23] that about 200 million hectares of forests are cleared annually for growing flowers for pets or processing food. A plate of vegetables uses only about 20 liters of water, whereas a plate of meat requires thousands of liters over long periods of farming and processing.

According to psychologists, animals in slaughterhouses,

23 Vũ Phượng, What does vegetarianism mean in Buddhism? Does it mean accumulating more virtue?
(Ăn chay trong Phật giáo có ý nghĩa gì, có phải tích đức nhiều hơn?)
https://thanhnien.vn/an-chay-trong-phat-giao-co-y-nghia-gi-co-phai-tich-duc-nhieu-hon-185230629123517591.htm

when killed for meat, experience anger, fear, anxiety, and unrest. They release toxins of resentment and hostility during that time. Consuming their meat can make humans susceptible to these negative emotional residues. Therefore, vegetarianism not only protects one's physical health but also maintains a clear, untainted mental state free from the emotional toxins of invaded food.

2.7. AHIMSA MAKES THE BODY HEALTHY WITH LESS DISEASE

In the Minor Sutta of Karma Discrimination, the Buddha told the young man Subha Todeyyaputta about the cause of illness being the karma of killing (himsa) as follows:

> Here, young man, there is a woman or a man who kills living beings, is cruel, has blood on his hands, has a mind dedicated to killing and injuring, and has no compassion for all kinds of living beings. Due to that karma, having achieved such success, achieved such achievements, after the body breaks up and dies, one is reborn in a realm of evil, in an evil destination, in the lower realms, in hell. If after the dissolution of the body and death, that person is not reborn in a realm of evil, in an evil realm, in a lower realm, in hell, if he can go to the human race, wherever he is born, he will have a short life. That path leads to a short life, young man, that is, killing, being cruel, having bloody hands, a mind dedicated to killing and injuring, and a mind that is not compassionate towards sentient beings.

But here, young man, there is a woman or a man who gives up killing, abstains from killing, gives up the staff, gives up the sword, knows how to be respectful, has compassion, and lives with compassion for the happiness of all living beings.

and sentient beings. Because of that karma, such success, such achievements, after the body breaks up and dies, that person is reborn in a good destination, the Heavenly World, in this world. If after the dissolution of the body and death, that person is not reborn in a good destination, in Heaven, in this world, if he goes to the human race, wherever he is born, he will have a long life. That path leads to longevity, young man, that is, giving up killing, staying away from killing, giving up the staff, giving up the sword, knowing how to cherish, having compassion, living compassionately to the happiness of all living beings and sentient beings.

Thus, illness is due to the habit (karma) of causing pain and harm to animals, and death when sick is due to the nature of being bloody and killing living beings. On the contrary, people with good karma such as being fond of living beings, being altruistic, and loving sentient beings will have little or no illness, be healthy and have a long life, and only through practice, only good karma, and changing karma can we save ourselves!

The blessing of the Precepts of Non-killing (ahimsa) can eliminate illnesses and fulfill aspirations as shown in the Sutta of Wishes (Middle Nikaya). The Buddha taught the benefits of keeping the precepts as follows:

"Bhikkhus, live fully in virtue, fully in the precepts, live protectively with the protection of the precepts, fully dignified and righteous, see the danger in small mistakes, accept correctly and study the precepts."

Monks, if a monk has the following wishes:

"May I be loved and respected by my fellow monks!"

"Hopefully I will receive items such as clothes, alms food, sleeping mats, and medicinal products!"

"May I now enjoy things such as clothes, alms foods, beds, and medicinal products! I hope that the actions of those who created those objects will have great retribution and great benefits!"

"May my blood relatives, when they die and think (of me) with joy (and thus) receive great retribution and great benefits!"

"I hope that I will conquer pleasure and non-pleasure, not that non-pleasure subdue me. I hope that my life will always be able to conquer my mind and not be disappointed!"

"May I conquer terror and fear, and not terror and fear conquer me! May I live always to conquer the fear and dread. That arise..."

That bhikkhu must perfect the precepts, persevere, have inner calm, uninterrupted meditation, achieve contemplation, and like to live in impure places, then the above wishes will be fulfilled.

The precepts are good dharma, the morality of everyone. Use good dharma to transform evil dharma. Evil is the karma of natural disasters, floods, fires, earthquakes, tsunamis, diseases, disasters, pandemics ...

Therefore, the Buddha taught that if we want to wish for peace, no illness, no accidents, want to be fully clothed, want to die and be reborn in a peaceful land, and want to control fear, each of us must take it seriously precepts, especially the precepts of non-killing (ahimsa). The Buddha's Dharma is very practical, specific, present and now. As a result, you will immediately see the fulfillment of your wishes from the power of maintaining the precepts.

2.8. AHIMSA IN KARMIC RETRIBUTION, THE LAW OF CAUSE AND EFFECT

Karma (Action): "Karma" refers to actions of the body (deeds), speech (words), and mind (intentions, thoughts, volition). "Outcome" denotes the consequences that follow karma, akin to a shadow following a form. By creating karma (whether good or bad), corresponding karmic results will be experienced (happiness, suffering).

Cause and Effect: The cause (seed), represents the effect (the fruit). Whatever seeds are sown will yield corresponding fruits. For example, sowing seeds of goodness leads to wholesome fruits, while sowing seeds of wrongdoing leads to encountering adversity, akin to planting mango seeds yielding mangoes and chili seeds yielding spicy chilies. This is the law of karmic causality, always operating according to its corresponding principles.

Cause: killing a pig and effect: a pig demanding his life.
(Image: Giác Ngộ Online)

In the Middle Length Discourses,[24] the Buddha teaches:

> With pure, supernormal vision, surpassing ordinary human sight, I see how beings come into existence and pass away. I discern whether they are noble or lowly, intelligent or dull, and how they are reborn according to their karma. I know clearly: those who have committed evil deeds in body, speech, or mind will, after the dissolution of the body, be reborn in suffering, in a bad destination, in hell. But those who have performed wholesome deeds in body, speech, or mind will be reborn in a good destination, in the heavenly realm.

24 Anguttara Nikāya. Chapter III – Three Dharmas. XI.The Enlightenment. Translated by the Most Ven. Thích Minh Châu.
https://www.budsas.org/uni/u-kinh-tangchibo/tangchi03-1116.htm

Similarly, if one sows seeds of nonviolence (ahimsa), one will be reborn in a good realm. Conversely, if one sows seeds of killing (himsa), and harming others, one will endure much suffering, and long-term torment in hell, as mentioned in the Samyutta Nikàya Sūtra[25] which tells the following story:

> Once, the Blessed One dwelled in Ràjagaha. At that time, Venerable Lakkhana and Venerable Moggallàna were dwelling on Mount Vulture Peak. Then Venerable Moggallàna, descending from Mount Vulture Peak, passed by a place and smiled.
>
> Seeing this, after finishing their meal, the two went to pay respects to the Blessed One. Venerable Lakkhana asked Venerable Moggallàna: For what reason, under what condition, did you smile upon descending from Mount Vulture Peak?

Using violent weapons to kill people, harm animals, will be punished and suffer in hell. (Image: Giác Ngộ Online)

> Venerable Lakkhana, when I descended from Mount Vulture Peak, I saw a skeleton floating in

25 Saṃyutta Nikāya (Tương Ưng Bộ Kinh) II, chapter 8, part 1, Piles of Bone [shortcut], published by Buddhist Studies in Vietnam Research Institute. 1993. p. 445.

the sky. Crows, vultures, and eagles were chasing and pecking at it, causing it great pain. Upon seeing this, I thought: "How marvelous! Such a person has become such a being, experiencing such suffering, undergoing such karma.

Then the Blessed One called the Bhikkhus and said: 'Those beings, O Bhikkhus, were a butcher of cattle in this Ràjagaha. Due to that person's well-practiced karma, after being cooked in hell for many years, many hundreds of years, many thousands of years, with the remainder of his karma, that person is experiencing the results with such a self now."

Through this story, we see the karmic consequences of actions such as killing sentient beings, especially the act of killing humans, which results in enduring immense suffering and long-term torment in hell.

The Śūraṅgama Sūtra,[26] teaches that after enduring suffering in hell, sentient beings with remaining karmic debts may be reborn as animals, hungry ghosts, or suffer again as humans, experiencing disabilities, illness, and painful conditions to repay the karmic debts from actions like killing and harming humans and animals. Past actions influence the present, and present actions affect the future.

Therefore, those who practice ahimsa, non-harming, can avoid negative karmic consequences and, by respecting and protecting life, practicing compassion, vegetarianism, and releasing life, they will receive good karmic rewards in this life and beyond.

---

26 The Śūraṅgama Sūtra. Chinese trans. by Pramiti. Vietnamese trans. by Tam Minh Le Dinh Tham.
Published by Phật Học Viện Quốc Tế. 1983.
https://ngaynay.vn/phatgiao/loi-phat-day-ve-qua-bao-dang-so-cua-nghiep-giet-hai-chung-sanh-post123743.html
https://www.huongsentemple.com/LuanHoiTrongLangKinhLangNghiem.pdf

2.9. AHIMSA IN THE JATAKA AND THE KHUDDHAKA NIKAYA

One day, the Venerable Punna requested permission from the Buddha to go to the violent and aggressive land of Surapatanta to use ahimsa to transform its people.[27]

> Bhikkhu Punna, you should know that Surapatanta is a distant, remote area. The people there are mostly rough, aggressive, and prone to violence. Those who come from other places often struggle to return with their lives intact. Now you wish to go there; I fear there might be danger for you!

Buddha and Venerable Punna. (Image: Giác Ngộ Online)

27 *The Stories of The Ten Great Disciples of the Buddha.*
The sources provided for this book are mainly the Tripitaka, the core of which is the Sutta Piṭaka, consisting of four sets: Dīgha Nikāya (Long Nikāya), Majjhima Nikāya (Middle Nikāya), Saṃyutta Nikāya (Samyutta Nikāya). Nikāya), and the Aṅguttara Nikāya (Aṅguttara Nikāya), especially the Etadaggavagga, part of the Anguttara Nikāya, in which the Buddha lists eighty "First Class" disciples. In addition, the Sutra Pitaka also has a collection of Khuddaka Nikāya (Small Nikāyas) in which there are two special collections, Theragāthā (The Elder Monks) and Therīgāthā (The Elder Nuns) telling about the practice life of the great disciples under verse form. Other famous sutras such as Jātaka (Buddha's Previous Birth Story), Dhammapada.
https://theravada.vn/dai-de-tu-phat-loi-gioi-thieu/
https://thuvienhoasen.org/a10416/03-ton-gia-phu-lau-na

But the Venerable Punna was determined and said:

> Blessed One! I am deeply grateful for your concern, but I wish to sacrifice myself, using the spirit of nonviolence (ahimsa) to transform them.

The Buddha, delighted by Punna's spirit of selflessness for the Dharma, continued to inquire further to encourage the assembly:

> Punna, you are right! As disciples of the Tathagata, it is crucial to make spreading the Dharma one of the essential aspects of our practice. However, if you go to Surapatanta and the people there do not accept your teachings but instead insult you, what will you do?
>
> Blessed One, if they only insult me, I would consider them still to be good people, for they have not yet resorted to physical violence.
>
> But what if they throw stones or beat you with sticks?
>
> Blessed One, I would still consider them good people, for they have not yet used knives or swords to cause me serious injury.
>
> But what if they use knives or swords to wound you severely?
>
> Blessed One, even then, I would consider them to have some goodness, for they have not yet brutally killed me.
>
> But what if they kill you?
>
> Blessed One, if this happens, I would be grateful to them, for by killing this physical body, they would be helping me attain Nirvana and allowing me to repay the deep kindness of the Blessed One. This would not be an obstacle for me; the important thing is that they see, even

> though they resort to violence (himsa) against me, I will respond with the spirit of ahimsa, nonviolence, and non-harm.
>
> The Buddha praised him:
>
> Punna, you are indeed a worthy disciple of the Tathagata. Whether in practice or in spreading the Dharma, you have embodied the qualities of patience and nonviolence (ahimsa) of the Tathagata. Your mind and environment are always calm and peaceful. Now you may go, and the Tathagata and the assembly will see you off.

Encouraged by the Buddha, the venerable Punna, deeply moved, steadfastly resolved to maintain ahimsa, unshaken by any circumstance. He paid homage to the Buddha and set off for Surapatanta...

2.10. THE BUDDHA USED AHIMSA TO RESOLVE THE WAR BETWEEN TWO TRIBES OVER A RIVER

Once, the Buddha was residing in the city of Savatthi. After the summer retreat, he heard the news about a conflict escalating to violence (himsa), where two tribes were using weapons to annihilate each other over a border river. The conflict was between two tribes ruled by two kings of the Shakya lineage, Emperor Mahanama and King Bhaddiya.

Buddha used loving speech and spirit Nonviolence for negotiation. (Image: Hoang Phap Pagoda)

Both tribes wanted to build dams to divert the river's flow to their own lands, making the water dispute even more intense. Ultimately, both nations had prepared their armies, ready for war. Upon hearing this, the Buddha decided to use the principle of ahimsa (nonviolence, harmlessness) to negotiate and prevent conflict, as both kings were his relatives.

The Buddha chose an appropriate place and invited both kings and their officials. He addressed them,[28] saying:

> During such a drought, the river's water is indeed very precious. But you must realize that there is something even more precious: the blood in your people's bodies. You cannot let a dispute over river water led to the spilling of your people's blood. Such an exchange is unwise and illogical. We fear famine and death from drought, but causing war brings death even faster.

Once the kings and their officials had understood his words, the Buddha continued gently: "The best solution now is to show mutual respect and share the remaining water equally. If the drought continues to the point where the river dries up, it must be understood as a common disaster that both nations must endure together. You should not be so heartless as to seek survival for yourselves at the cost of the other's death.

However, the situation was not as dire as it seemed. According to historical records, the river had never run dry because it originated from the abundant Himalayan mountains. Both tribes were encouraged to endure patiently in friendship, which would make the issue much more manageable.

After listening to the Buddha's wise mediation, both tribes transformed their hatred into forgiveness and shared resources

28 Doan Trung Con compiled and edited by Nguyen Minh Tien. *The Story of Shakyamuni Buddha* (Truyện Phật Thích-ca). Third act. 48. The Buddha made Peace and ended the War between Two Countries https://www.adidaphat.net/pubs/kinhdien.aspx?ID=1004

like brothers. They happily laid down their weapons and swords, ceasing their violent conflict, and agreed to share the water fairly.

Indeed, the drought did not dry up the river. Thanks to the Buddha's mediation using the principle of ahimsa as a foundation for peace, the potential for a bloody war was averted.

Buddha used ahimsa to reconcile both sides.
(Image: Giác Ngộ Online)

The Khuddaka Nikàya also recounts as follows: The Rohini River flowed between the cities of Kapilavatthu and Koliya, with a single dam that allowed people from both sides to have water for agriculture. Around May to June, when the river's water level was low and the rice was starting to blossom, people from both sides grew anxious. If both sides drew water into their fields, the Rohini River would not have enough to supply both. This led to a heated argument, with neither side willing to compromise, ultimately leading to physical altercations. The leaders got involved, and the kings of both sides began to compete for the river's water with weapons. The Buddha, upon hearing this, personally went to the border of the two nations to mediate. When the people saw the Buddha, they laid down their weapons. The Buddha asked:

What is more precious: the river water, the land, or human lives? The kings replied:

Lord, human lives are the most precious. The Buddha said:

Then why are you destroying each other over a little water?

The Buddha then explained that human life is more valuable than any material possession in the world. The kings and the people, realizing the truth, were pleased with each other and ceased fighting.[29]

2.11. THE BUDDHA'S TEACHING ON WAR AND VICTORY

Buddha analyzes the consequences of winning and losing. (Image: Giác Ngộ Online)

The Sūtra of Two Statements About War[30] recounts that once, King Pasenadi of Kosala waged war against his nephew, King Ajātasattu of Magadha, and suffered a defeat. When the

29 Khuddaka Nikāya (Tiểu Bộ), Sutta 536, The Story of the Bird Lord Kunāla (Chuyện Chúa Chim Kunāla). https://thuvienhoasen.org/a30192/duc-phat-thich-ca-bieu-tinh-bat-bao-dong-

30 Suttanipata (Kinh Tập). Chapter 3: Samyutta Kosala. II: Chapter Two 3.14–15. Two Words About War (Hai Lời Nói Về Chiến Tranh).

Buddha learned of this fratricidal conflict, he taught:

Victory breeds hatred,
Defeat brings suffering.
The wise stay peaceful,
Abandoning both victory and defeat.

Later, King Pasenadi amassed a stronger army and fought against King Ajātasattu again, this time emerging victorious. He captured King Ajātasattu along with all his soldiers, elephants, and chariots. When the Buddha heard of this, he taught:

Out of self-interest,
One attacks and harms others.
When others retaliate,
Suffering begets more suffering.
The fool thinks this way,
When evil has not yet ripened.
But when evil has ripened,
The fool endures suffering.
Killing leads to being killed,
Victory leads to being defeated,
Cursing leads to being cursed,
Harming others leads to being harmed.
Thus the cycle of karma unfolds,
Harm begets more harm.

The cycles of victory and defeat, ups and downs, and gains and losses all revolve around the law of cause and effect. It is best to use compassion (ahimsa) to end the pain and suffering of war.

---

https://suttacentral.net/sn3.14/vi/minh_chau?lang=en&reference=none&highlight=false

2.12. THE BANDIT ANGULIMALA BECOMES A SAINT OF AHIMSA

The Buddha's disciples came from all walks of life, including the courtesan Ambapali, the outcast Upali, and the bandit Angulimala. All were accepted equally into the Sangha and attained enlightenment. Notably, Angulimala, who had lived a life of violence, robbery, and the murder of innocent people, was transformed by the Buddha's teachings. He became a virtuous monk, a pure saint, capable of blessing and bringing happiness to those in distress.

The story of Angulimala, the bandit who killed 999 people and later attained Arahantship,[31] unfolds as follows:

Under the reign of King Pasenadi in the Kingdom of Kosala, there was a bandit who followed the misguided teachings of his corrupt teacher. He was told that by cutting off exactly 1,000 fingers, he would gain supernatural powers and become an exceptional Brahmin. From a gentle young man, he turned into a murderer, killing people without a second thought. After each murder, he cut off a finger as proof, strung them together, dried them, and wore them around his neck. Thus, he earned the name Angulimala, which means "Garland of Fingers" or "the bandit who kills and wears a necklace of fingers."

This horrific situation caused immense fear and anxiety among the people of Kosala. Villages became deserted, towns were abandoned, and the kingdom was left in disarray. King Pasenadi himself sought an audience with the Buddha, informing Him of his plan to personally lead his army to capture Angulimala.

On that day, the Buddha was in a deep meditative state of

31 Angulimala: From a bandit who killed 999 people to an arhat who attained sainthood.
Angulimālasuttavannanā, Majjhimapannāsa, Angulimālasuttavannanā
https://chuabavang.com/angulimala-tu-mot-ten-tuong-cuop-giet-999-mang-nguoi-cho-den-bac-a-la-han-dac-thanh-qua-d4946.html

great compassion. After surveying sentient beings with whom He had karmic ties, He saw Angulimala. The Buddha knew that Angulimala was inherently gentle, honest, and virtuous but had been led astray by his misguided teacher into a life of crime.

The Buddha also realized that a few words of guidance from Him would be enough to awaken pure faith in Angulimala. He would then renounce his sinful actions, repent, observe the precepts, and eventually attain the holy path and fruits of arahantship along with profound wisdom.

The robber let go of his mother's hand and chased after the Buddha. (Image: Giác Ngộ Online)

At that time, the garland around Angulimala's neck had reached 999 fingers, leaving him only one finger short of fulfilling his goal. He thought of killing just one more person to complete his collection and gain his teacher's secret knowledge to become an exceptional Brahmin.

Suddenly, Angulimala heard his mother's voice calling out in the forest. He turned and thought about killing his own mother to obtain the last finger. However, as he approached, he saw the serene figure of the Buddha (who had manifested there to save Angulimala) calmly walking. Angulimala decided to kill the Buddha instead of his mother.

But something extraordinary happened. No matter how hard Angulimala ran to catch up with the Buddha, he could not reach Him. The distance between them remained the same.

Frustrated, Angulimala shouted, "Hey, monk, why don't you stop when I call you?"

The Buddha calmly replied, "Angulimala, I have already stopped. It is you who have not yet stopped."

The robber ran but could not catch up to the Buddha even though the Buddha stood still. (Image: Giác Ngộ Online)

Angulimala continued:

> Everywhere people say that the monks of the Sakya clan always speak the truth, that their words never contradict their actions. But why, when I call out to you as you walk, do you say that you have stopped? And yet I, who have stopped, you say have not stopped?

The Buddha replied calmly, "Angulimala, I stopped long ago (I ceased doing evil, became ahimsa, nonviolent long ago). It is you who have not yet stopped (you have not ceased your violent and murderous ways, himsa)."

Upon hearing these words, Angulimala suddenly paused. It

was as if a light had dawned in his mind, enlightening him: "I have plunged too deeply into sin, killing too many people, but all I have seen is the fear and suffering of others. This is not the path to happiness for the many, but a path of crime. I must stop, like the Blessed One."

At that moment, Angulimala slowly placed his sword on the ground and knelt before the Buddha with hands folded in reverence: "Venerable Sir, I realize my sins now! You have personally come to this forest for my long-term happiness and peace. You have compassionately helped me step out of the darkness, ignorance, and evil deeds. From now on, I vow to permanently renounce violence and bloodshed. Please witness my sincere and earnest repentance! Venerable Sir, please allow me to become a monk and follow your path of compassion!"

The robber puts down his sword (himsa) surrendering to the Buddha's path of ahimsa. (Image: Giác Ngộ Online)

From that point on, Angulimala was ordained by the Buddha, joined the monastic order, and practiced the Dharma. Although at times, due to the power of his past evil karma, he was stoned, beaten, and left bleeding with torn robes by people, he remained calm and patient, continuing his practice with the monastic community until he attained the state of an Arahant.

When King Pasenadi learned that Angulimala had become a monk, he respectfully folded his hands in reverence and bowed to him (even though he had previously organized an army to capture Angulimala).

The Blessing of the Monk Angulimala for Pregnant Women

The vow to bring happiness to sentient beings by the Venerable Angulimala began when he joined the monastic order. One day, as the Venerable Angulimala was on his alms round in the village, he suddenly heard the cries of a woman who was in labor but unable to give birth. There were no doctors around, and he feared that both the mother and child might not survive. Witnessing this distressing scene, the Venerable Angulimala hurried back to the monastery and reported to the Buddha:

> Venerable Sir, I encountered a woman in labor, struggling to give birth and in great pain. Please, Venerable Sir, show me how I can help her safely.

At that time, the Buddha instructed:

> Angulimala, go to the woman and make a truthful vow: 'Since I was born, I have not intentionally taken the life of any living being. By this truth, may you safely give birth to your child, and may your child be safe as well.

Upon hearing this, the Venerable Angulimala hesitated, wondering if he would be lying since he had previously killed many people. But the Buddha compassionately explained:

> Angulimala, since you were born into the noble lineage of the Dharma (since you were

ordained).

Following the Buddha's instruction, Angulimala went to the woman in labor and made the vow:

> Since I was born (ordained), I have not intentionally taken the life of any living being. By this truth, may you safely give birth to your child, and may your child be safe as well!

Angulimala, adhering to the Buddha's words, made a truthful vow to transfer merit to the woman in dire straits. As soon as he finished his vow, the cries of a newborn were heard, demonstrating the miraculous and profound effect of the Venerable Angulimala's truthful vow and virtuous nature. Subsequently, the Venerable Angulimala diligently practiced and attained the Four Noble Truths, achieving the state of an Arahant with transcendent wisdom.

Angulimala followed the Buddha's instructions to make a truthful vow to bestow blessings upon the woman in peril. As soon as his words were spoken, the cries of a newborn baby were heard, demonstrating the miraculous and profound effect of the Venerable Angulimala's truthful vow and virtuous nature. Subsequently, the Venerable Angulimala diligently practiced, realized the Four Noble Truths, and attained the state of an Arahant with transcendent wisdom.

Through this story, we see that the Buddha's teachings are egalitarian and non-discriminatory, regardless of race or evil deeds. The Buddha used ahimsa (nonviolence) to transform those who practiced himsa (violence). As a result, those who once practiced himsa became ahimsa saints, pure and capable of protecting others.

Therefore, Buddhism encourages the use of education, not hatred, fear, avoidance, or capital punishment, to deal with wrongdoers. This world is full of suffering, wrong views, and violence. Only the Dharma, with its principle of ahimsa, can save sentient beings from the ocean of suffering and lead them to the shore of enlightenment.

We should transform and negotiate in accordance with the truth and the conditions to change individuals and society. With the great compassion and wisdom of the Buddha, even an extremely evil person like Angulimala was transformed into a kind and later revered Saint. This is reflected in the saying: "Turn your head, and you will see the shore."

Why did the Venerable Angulimala possess the power to ensure the safety of pregnant women? There is a saying: "The past may be that of a bandit, but the present can be that of a saint. Conversely, the past may be saintly, but the present could be of a bandit." Thus, nothing is fixed; the current actions determine a person's character. Everything is created by the mind, as illustrated by the following verse:

Sins arise from the mind,

and repentance must be from the mind.

Once the mind is eradicated, sins will disappear.

When sins disappear and the mind is eradicated, everything is empty.

This is the true essence of repentance.

Leaving the past of violence (himsa) behind, from the day he ordained, the monk Angulimala wholeheartedly repented, ceased his evil actions (just as the Buddha had ceased), and purified himself by adhering to the precepts of non-harm (ahimsa), truthfulness, and many other virtues. The precepts possess a powerful and miraculous ability, enabling one to bestow this power upon others. Thus, the pregnant woman and her child were safe and healthy, and the monk became a useful and revered figure in society.

2.13. THE BUDDHA TEACHES SEVEN FACTORS FOR A PROSPEROUS NATION

After mediating and preventing the bloody conflict between Emperor Maha-Nama and King Good Perception over the river dispute, the Buddha continued to serve as a spiritual advisor to King Ajātasattu. He introduced seven factors for the prosperity of a nation without violence (himsa) as follows:

Buddha taught how to get rich on the basis of harmony and mutual respect. (Image: Giác Ngộ Online)

"One time, the Buddha was residing on Vulture Peak Mountain, near the city of Rajgir, along with a congregation of 1,250 great monks. At that time, King Ajātasattu of the kingdom of Magadha desired to invade the Vajji confederation with weapons of war. He sent his minister, Vassakara, to consult the Buddha on this matter.

At that moment, Ananda was standing behind the Buddha, fanning him. The Buddha asked Ananda seven questions:

> Buddha: "Ananda, have you heard that the Vajji regularly gather to discuss and make decisions on righteous matters?"
>
> Ananda: "Yes, I have heard."
>
> Buddha: "If they continue to do so, they will prosper and remain secure for a long time, and no

harm will come to them."

Buddha: "Ananda, have you heard that the Vajji live in harmony and respect their leaders, and the leaders respect the people?"

Ananda: "Yes, I have heard."

Buddha: "If they continue to do so, they will prosper and remain secure for a long time, and no harm will come to them."

Buddha: "Ananda, have you heard that the Vajji respect and uphold their laws and traditions, understanding what is forbidden and not deviating from proper conduct?"

Ananda: "Yes, I have heard."

Buddha: "If they continue to do so, they will prosper and remain secure for a long time, and no harm will come to them."

Buddha: "Ananda, have you heard that the Vajji respect and care for their parents and honor their elders and teachers?"

Ananda: "Yes, I have heard."

Buddha: "If they continue to do so, they will prosper and remain secure for a long time, and no harm will come to them."

Buddha: "Ananda, have you heard that the Vajji respect and honor their shrines and spirits?"

Ananda: "Yes, I have heard."

Buddha: "If they continue to do so, they will prosper and remain secure for a long time, and no harm will come to them."

Buddha: "Ananda, have you heard that the Vajji maintain purity and decency within their households, avoiding misconduct even in their entertainment and speech?"

Ananda: "Yes, I have heard."

Buddha: "If they continue to do so, they will prosper and remain secure for a long time, and no harm will come to them."

Buddha: "Ananda, have you heard that the Vajji respect, support, and associate closely with monks and those who uphold moral conduct?"

Ananda: "Yes, I have heard."

Buddha: "If they continue to do so, they will prosper and remain secure for a long time, and no harm will come to them."

At this point, Minister Vassakara respectfully addressed the Buddha:

Vassakara: "If the people of Vajji practice even one of these principles, it would be difficult to defeat them, let alone all seven. Given the importance of state affairs, I now take my leave to return."

The Buddha then remarked:

Buddha: "One should know the right time."

Vassakara then stood up, circled the Buddha three times, bowed, and departed.[32]

Through this dialogue, we can see that the Buddha placed great emphasis on building a peaceful, prosperous, and wealthy society by ensuring that the people of that nation:

1. Engage in democratic activities,
2. Foster national solidarity,
3. Uphold the rule of law,
4. Maintain harmony across generations,

32 Dìghàgama (Kinh Trường A-hàm). Sutra Wandering (Kinh Du hành).

5. Respect women,
6. Honor various beliefs,
7. Value and support wise and virtuous individuals.

These principles reflect a comprehensive approach to creating a stable and flourishing community. By promoting democratic participation, legal integrity, and respect for all members of society, the Buddha's teachings guide us toward a more just and harmonious world.

2.14. THE BUDDHA USED THE SPIRIT OF EQUALITY AND NONVIOLENCE (AHIMSA) TO CHANGE SOCIETY

Four classes of racism in ancient Indian society. (Image: Internet)

More than 2,600 years ago, ancient Indian society was characterized by numerous castes, with four main castes:

Brahmins (priests of Hinduism): Believed to be born from the mouth of Brahma, thus considered noble.

Chinese trans. by Buddhayaśsa. Vietnamese trans. by the Most Ven. Tue Sy. https://phatgiaodongnai.org/7-phap-giup-quoc-gia-hung-thinh.html

Kshatriyas (warriors and rulers): Born from the arms of Brahma.

Vaishyas (merchants and farmers): Born from the thighs of Brahma.

Shudras (servants and laborers): Born from the feet of Brahma, thus regarded as lowly and inferior.

The caste system was a fundamental principle of social life in ancient India. Each person's caste was determined entirely by their lineage and family background, passed down from generation to generation (ideology). No circumstances, academic achievements, or efforts could change a person's caste throughout their life. This system was dominated by the Brahmins.

People blindly accepted this system, living in injustice, oppression, and inequality, believing that someone born from Brahma's feet was destined to be lowly and subservient for life, while someone born from Brahma's mouth was a Brahmin, revered by all regardless of their actions, words, or thoughts.

The Buddha made significant contributions to countering caste discrimination in India. He advocated for equality, nonviolence (ahimsa), and the idea that actions and karma could change a person's status. It was unreasonable to think anyone was born inherently lowly or noble. One's actions and karma determined their status.

In the opening verses of the Brahmajala Sūtra and many other Mahayana Sūtras, the Buddha emphasized, "I am a Buddha already enlightened; you are Buddhas yet to be enlightened," "All beings have Buddha nature,[33]" and "There is no caste in tears and blood which are equally salty and red." Regardless of skin color, academic achievements, appearance, or wealth, social status is equal. The Buddha implemented this idea by accepting everyone from all castes, whether considered high or

33 Brahmajāla Sutta: The All-embracing Net of Views. Translated from the Pali by Bhikkhu Bodhi. 2010. Alternate translation: Thanissaro.

low, into his Sangha.

With the foundation of the teachings of equality and nonviolence, the Buddha converted thousands of outcasts, slaves, and lower-caste individuals to the Triple Gem (Buddha, Dharma, Sangha), with nearly 1,250 people ordaining into the monastic order. Even women, who were seen as inferior in that society, were allowed to ordain and join the Buddha's disciples,[34] enjoying the same freedom and enlightenment.

Therefore, the Buddha admitted people like the barber Upāli, the courtesan Ambapālī, and the bandit Angulimāla, all from the lowest Shudra caste, into the ranks of his noble disciples, surprising many kings and nobles of the time.

To illustrate the severe social prejudices, here is the story of Venerable Ānanda asking for water from a low-caste girl:[35]

https://www.accesstoinsight.org/tipitaka/dn/dn.01.0.bodh.html
https://www.daotranglienhoa.com/wp-content/uploads/2023/08/kinh_pham_vong.pdf

34 Six Point of Reverent Harmonies:
1. The Harmony in Deed means that in terms of daily activities in an organization, we live together in a group and should often take care and help each other.
2. The Harmony in Speech without Fighting, in terms of communication and advice through language and words, always show the spirit of encouraging and advising each other to do good and stop doing evil.
3. The Harmony in Outlook means standing on the ideological level, always respecting and loving other people's opinions. If that opinion is right, if not, then let's discuss together, figure it out, and happily accept.
4. The Harmony in Morality means that we live together in a group, we should always follow and practice together according to the common precepts that have been set.
5. The Harmony in Views is the understanding gained about the truth, or the principle that has been understood and would like to share with everyone, to practice together.
6. The Harmony in Economics is that all material wealth obtained from the donations of donors are legally divided equally.
In Buddhism, the Six Harmonies are six areas where Buddhist practitioners should be respectful and work in harmony with one another. The list of these six areas varies among Buddhist texts, but they can include:
action, word, mind, observance of the precepts, doctrinal views, and practice.

35 Minh Duc Trieu Tam Anh, A lowly caste girl felt in love Venerable Ānanda: *One Life, One Sun and Moon* (Một cuộc đời, Một vầng nhật nguyệt).

One day, Venerable Ānanda was traveling far away. On his way back to Jetavana Monastery, he went on his alms round in the outskirts of a village and then rested under a tree to have his meal. After finishing his meal, he went along a path looking for water to drink in a poor village at the foot of a mountain. Seeing a young girl drawing water from a well, he approached and stood silently beside her with his alms bowl in hand, looking down.

The girl, named Prakirti, was from the lowly outcast Chandala caste, living on the outskirts of society. When she saw a "Brahmin" of noble appearance standing silently nearby, she became very frightened. She bowed her head and whispered:

Sir, do you need something?

Venerable Ānanda, still looking down, stated his purpose:

Dear sister, please give me some water.

The girl, even more terrified that a person from a high caste would speak to her, replied:

I am lowly.

I only need some water.

I am of the lowest caste. No one drinks our water.

I just need a little water to quench my thirst. Water is for washing, cleaning, and drinking; it has no caste distinction.

Hearing this strange statement about no caste distinction from the stranger, the girl felt bolder and looked up to respond clearly:

I am a girl of the lowly Chandala caste. This well water is clear and sweet, but to those of higher castes, it is considered impure and dirty. Only we drink it. People of higher castes regard it as unclean and will not drink it, let alone use it to wash

---

Episode 6. Publishing House: Văn Học. 2014.
Minh Đức Triều Tâm Ảnh, Cô Gái Hạ Tiện Yêu Tôn Giả Ānanda: Một cuộc đời, Một vầng nhật nguyệt. Tập 6. Nhà xuất bản Văn Học. 2014.
https://thuvienhoasen.org/a21264/co-gai-ha-tien-yeu-ton-gia-nanda

their hands.

I did not ask which caste you belong to. I only asked for water.

In this land, broadly speaking, there are two castes: the high and the low. I belong to the lowest caste in society.

I do not care about your caste. I just need some water.

How can I dare to offer you water? I am a lowly girl. People living in grand, noble palaces belong to higher castes. People like us cannot even look at them. They detest even stepping on our shadows. When we come near, they avoid us. If they are forced to see us, they must wash their faces and purify themselves with scented water, while grimacing and lamenting, 'Oh gods! What did I just see? A lowly person!' So how can I dare to offer you water? How can I dare to come close to offer it? If my shadow touches you, you would become a lowly person too!

Venerable Ānanda felt indignant about the terrible prejudices of society and pitied the low-caste people living in such unjust and humiliating conditions. He wanted to clarify to the girl the concept of equality among people according to the teachings of his Master:

> "I do not pay attention to so-called high and low castes. I only know that you are a human being, just like me. I have never heard that caste can create a difference between one person and another. I do not accept such outdated, barbaric, and skewed ideas. All of us have two hands, two legs, two eyes, one mouth, one face, and one nose. Can the sun rise in the west for those of a lower caste? Can the sun rise in the east only for the upper castes? Furthermore, feelings of happiness and suffering are the same for everyone. When we eat, everyone's stomachs get full and expand; when we are hungry, everyone's stomachs grumble and shrink! So how are we different,

dear sister?"

Indeed, between humans, everyone is the same, Prakirti grasped the very egalitarian and open-minded view of the "stranger" but wanted to understand more clearly:

> Outwardly, there isn't much difference, as you have said. But those of the higher castes are born into their noble lineage because of their good karma. We, on the other hand, are born into this low caste because of our bad karma and many sins. They are blessed to be born from the mouth or shoulders of Mahā Brahma, while we are 'unfortunately' born from his feet or heels. We are not allowed to learn the Vedas. Therefore, we are ignorant, inferior, and deprived in all respects. We are not considered part of any caste, being at the very bottom of society.
>
> My Master does not teach such things. He teaches that we are all equal, without caste in our blood and tears. Everyone's blood is red and everyone's tears are salty. You may listen as I recite this teaching from my Master:
>
> 'No jaccā vasalo hoti
>
> Na jaccā hoti brāhmaṇo
>
> Kammanā vasalo hoti
>
> Kammanā hoti brāhmaṇo.'

It means: "No one is born a low-caste person. No one is born a Brahmin. It is through their actions that one becomes low-caste. It is through their actions that one becomes a Brahmin.

The girl felt deeply moved as if she had drunk in the refreshing words. She cautiously looked around to see if anyone was watching. With a mixture of fear and embarrassment, she lowered her eyes, and with trembling hands, poured water from the bucket into the bowl. Once there was enough water,

Venerable Ānanda lifted the bowl and drank deeply. Afterward, he gently explained further to her, emphasizing the following:

> 'You must recognize the value of a person within the human community. Do not feel inferior or live according to society's imposed regulations. You must respect the inherent worth within yourself, rise, stand tall, and maintain the noble qualities of being human. Humans are inherently equal and free! No law, institution, society, or individual has the right to take away that equality and freedom.'

Balance of Justice - Fairness. (Image: Internet)

Through this story, it is evident that Buddha Shakyamuni was a social revolutionary and a revolutionary thinker who asserted that everyone is equal; it is only through actions that one determines whether they are lowly or noble.

Buddha and his monastic community successfully liberated people from the shackles of the caste system dominated by Brahmins, using the principles of "equality" and "nonviolence" (ahimsa). This was a key cornerstone towards creating a peaceful and free society. The path and revolutionary methods of the Blessed One can be said to have been ahead of his time and pioneering for subsequent revolutionary movements, even up to modern times.

CHAPTER 3

EMPEROR ASOKA'S USE OF THE PRINCIPLE OF AHIMSA TO GOVERN THE COUNTRY

3.1. EMPEROR AŚOKA'S BELLICOSE NATURE AND THE INVASION OF KALINGA

Emperor Aśoka and the battle of Kalinga. (Image: Internet)

Emperor Aśoka (Asoka, Ashoka, 304-232 BCE), one of the greatest rulers of ancient India, ruled over the vast and wealthy Mauryan Empire. The emperor often engaged in military campaigns to expand his territories. One of the final battles took place in Kalinga, located on the eastern coast of India (modern-day Orissa), resulting in the brutal deaths of over 100,000 Kalinga civilians and the capture of 150,000 as prisoners of war.

3.2. EMPEROR AŚOKA'S EDICTS ON BUDDHIST NONVIOLENCE

While his soldiers celebrated the victory with a feast, Emperor Aśoka walked alone along the Kalinga River, still flowing with the innocent people's spilled blood and scattered flesh... Suddenly, the king awakened to the enormity of his sins and resolved to return to the path of righteousness, upholding the principle of nonviolence (ahimsa) as ancient sages had said, "discard the weapons, establish the Dharma" (abandoning weapons, thereby establishing the path to enlightenment). Thus, from a cruel and bloodthirsty ruler, he transformed into a compassionate and virtuous Buddhist monarch. From conquests achieved through swords, daggers, guns, and weapons, the king sought a spiritual transformation through the principle of ahimsa, winning the hearts of others through Buddhist teachings, just as the Buddha had practiced for 49 years of preaching and salvation. A king's edict states:

> Eight years after his coronation, King Priyadarsinda (Emperor Aśoka) conquered the territory of Kalinga. One hundred and fifty thousand people were deported, one hundred thousand people died in battles, and many more died in even greater numbers. After the conquest of Kalinga, now is the time to enthusiastically apply the precepts, to respect the precepts, to obey the instructions recorded in the precepts applied throughout the kingdom of Emperor Aśoka. There is no forgiveness for regret, after

conquering Kalinga. Indeed, conquering an independent country is a murderous act, causing scenes of massacre and deportation for many people: these thoughts now appear strongly and torment Emperor Aśoka...[36]

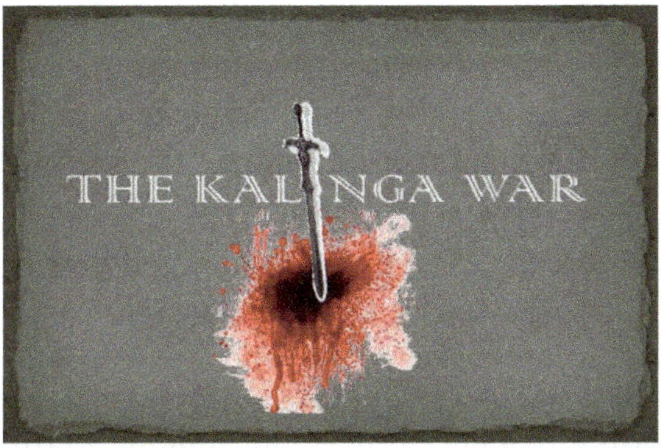

Sea of blood in the Kalinga war. (Image: Internet)

From that moment, Aśoka reformed, took refuge in the Triple Gem, built temples, supported the Sangha, and erected stupas, stone inscriptions, and pillars at the sacred sites associated with the Buddha. He governed his people based on the compassionate and wise principles of Buddhism, especially the principle of non-harm (ahimsa). He sent many Buddhist missions to spread the Dharma in Sri Lanka, Thailand, and even the western Greek kingdoms around 250 BCE. This effort significantly contributed to the widespread dissemination of Buddhism globally, lasting to the present day. He intended to persuade rulers of neighboring countries to abandon their ambitions of conquering others through warfare and instead establish peaceful and stable kingdoms grounded in the principle of ahimsa.

36 Dr. Hoàng Phong, Aśoka – A Buddhist King (A Dục, Một Vị Vua Phật Tử).
https://quangduc.com/a27860/a-duc-mot-vi-vua-phat-tu-hoang-phong

3.3. NONVIOLENCE (AHIMSA) AS THE PRINCIPAL GOVERNANCE OF EMPEROR AŚOKA

Nonviolence became the way of life and governance for Emperor Aśoka. It can be said that this was the king's repentance after the bloody massacre in Kalinga. In the first decree issued by the emperor across almost the entire Mauryan Empire, he banned the killing of living beings (ahimsa) in daily life, including the slaughter of animals for sacrifices and meat consumption.[37]

In the thirteenth edict, the king narrated that following the victory in Kalinga, which resulted in massive casualties among civilians and soldiers, he was deeply remorseful. This regret tormented his conscience, and he earnestly wished for all people to have the right to a peaceful, stable, and moral life (dhamma). Emperor Aśoka hoped that people would also repent, put down their swords (abandon violent actions as they did in the past), and cease killing (both in the present and future).

Emperor Aśoka declared, "Only the victory of Dharma (the Law) is the true and supreme victory; everyone benefits from such a victory, leading to peace and prosperity."

Emperor Aśoka embodied the spirit of ahimsa (nonviolence) by abolishing the death penalty within his kingdom. As recorded in the Kalinga Edict:

"Just as I wish for my own children to enjoy all happiness and peace in this life and the next, I also wish the same happiness and peace for all people.

There have been instances where some individuals were imprisoned without any justifiable reason, causing immense

---

37 K. R. Norman, *Buddhism and Aśoka King* (Phật Giáo và A-dục Vương). Collection of articles about King Aśoka and Vietnamese trans by Nguyên Tâm. https://quangduc.com/a27861/Aśoka-cuoc-doi-va-su-nghiep-tuyen-tap-cac-bai-viet-ve-vua-a-duc

suffering to many others. Therefore, you must follow the path of nonviolence (ahimsa) and moderation. However, this path of peace cannot be pursued if you remain enslaved to vices such as envy, impatience, cruelty, haste, superficiality, laziness, and passivity.

Do not succumb to these negative traits. This decree is inscribed here to ensure that the magistrates in the city refrain from imprisoning people without just cause. Furthermore, for this purpose, every five years, I send out envoys on missions. These envoys must demonstrate kindness, compassion, and respect for the sacredness of all life."[38]

Thus, we see that Emperor Aśoka's approach to governance involved treating his subjects with the same care and affection as his children. If children made mistakes, they were to be taught with love and compassion, not through extreme and violent measures such as harsh punishments or execution. Magistrates were expected to be fair and just, avoiding unnecessary imprisonment and bureaucracy, and instead using peaceful methods to educate and guide the people.

In another edict, Aśoka also issued a decree for the Mauryan Empire and neighboring regions to practice ahimsa towards animals, establishing hospitals for the care of animals and pets:

"Throughout my kingdom and in neighboring territories, such as the lands of the Cholas, Pandyas, Satyaputras, and Keralaputras, on the island of Tambapanni (Sri Lanka), in the kingdom of Greek King Antiochus, and the neighboring realms of Antiochus, I have established two types of hospitals—one for humans and one for animals."

The author Copleston, in his book *Buddhism Theravada and Present*, acknowledges that "The credit for establishing the first hospitals undoubtedly belongs to Buddhism." It should be added that besides the first hospitals for people, Emperor Aśoka also built hospitals for animals! The earliest hospital built by

38 Ibid.

Westerners was the hospital Diu in Paris (France) in the 7th century CE, which is about 1,000 years after Aśoka's hospitals.

Emperor Aśoka's love and commitment to nonviolence (ahimsa) towards animals were truly exceptional, as: "No animal shall be slaughtered or sacrificed anymore."

3.4. THE DHARMA PRACTICE OF KING AŚOKA

King Aśoka was a devout Buddhist, a righteous ruler, deeply advocating the spirit of ahimsa (nonviolence). He used Buddhist teachings to govern his country and propagate Buddhism to foreign lands, as described in various practices[39] such as dhammathambhas "pillars of dhamma," dhammalipi "inscriptions of dhamma," dhammamgala "rites of dhamma," dhammadàna "gifts of dhamma," dhammanuggaha "protection of dhamma," dhammayàtras "journeys of dhamma," dhammasavana "listening to dhamma," dhammamahàmàtras "ministers of dhamma," dhammavijaya "victory through dhamma," etc.

Therefore, Aśoka is honored as the renowned Dharma King, forever linked with the history of Indian Buddhism, especially the principle of ahimsa. King Aśoka continues to live on in humanity's memory, and Buddhist history acknowledges him with gratitude, as evidenced by this passage:

"In the history of the world, there have been thousands of kings and emperors who called themselves "their Highnesses," "their Majesties," "Their Exalted Majesties," and so on. They shone for a brief moment and quickly faded away. But King Aśoka continues to shine brightly like a radiant star, even to this day."[40]

39 Ibid.

40 H.G. Wells (1866–1946), *A Short History of the World.* 1922. https://thuvienhoasen.org/a23735/dai-de-a-duc-mot-ong-vua-ho-tri-phat-phap

King Aśoka supports the promotion of Buddhism.
(Image: Giác Ngộ Online)

CHAPTER 4

SOCIAL LEADERS APPLYING AHIMSA IN THE MODERN ERA

4.1. MAHATMA GANDHI (1869-1948)

Mohandas Karamchand Gandhi is revered as a saint (Mahatma means saint, great, noble soul), a politician, a revolutionary activist, and the leader of the Indian National Congress who applied the principle of "nonviolence" (ahimsa) as the most peaceful and powerful weapon in the resistance movement against British colonial rule.

Born into a prestigious and influential family, M.K. Gandhi received a thorough education. He became a lawyer in Bombay after graduating from law school in the United Kingdom. Around 1893, he went to South Africa to work as a legal advisor for an Indian trading firm. Witnessing the racial discrimination policies of British colonialists against Indians and South Africans, M.K. Gandhi stood up to lead the community with the method of "Satyagraha" (which means courageously practicing nonviolence (ahimsa) and truth.

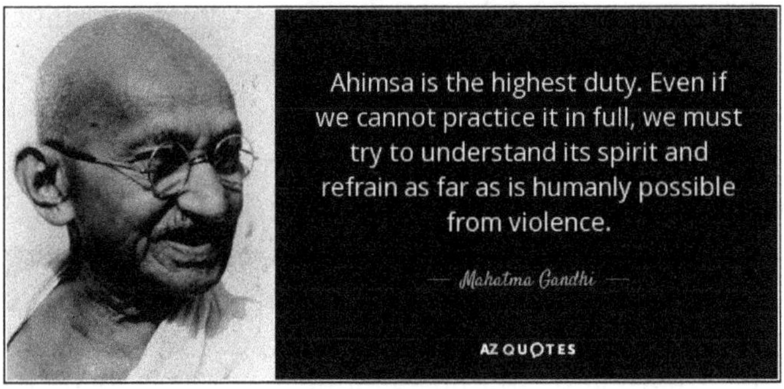

At the beginning of 1915, M.K. Gandhi returned to his homeland, and in 1919, he became the leader of the Indian National Congress, a major political party in India. After World War I, the British implemented the harsh and brutal Rowlatt Act in India. Under M.K. Gandhi's leadership, people all over India rose against the colonialists with the slogan: "Do or die? Courageously, they refrained from using weapons like guns and knives and instead employed nonviolent actions such as boycotts, civil disobedience, resolutely refusing to use British goods, not cooperating with the government, not enlisting in the British army, and the Salt March (protesting the British salt monopoly law).

M.K. Gandhi's revolutionary life was fraught with trials, dangers, hardships, and multiple imprisonments by the British colonists. However, all the enemy's tactics could not subdue Gandhi's spirit, wisdom, compassion, and courage. Ultimately, on August 15, 1947, the British colonizers were forced to grant independence to India.

"Non-harming" (ahimsa) is a fundamental and paramount precept of Buddhism and Jainism. M.K. Gandhi effectively, widely, and successfully employed ahimsa to such an extent that the entire Indian population adopted it as a peaceful weapon in the movement to gain freedom and independence from British colonial rule, without causing injury or loss of life. Consequently, the people of India revered the principle of ahimsa as the embodiment of M.K. Gandhi's ideology, "Gandhism. "He was honored as Saint Gandhi (Mahatma Gandhi): "A saint among politicians and a politician among saints."[41]

The father of India's independence, Mahatma Gandhi, preached and practiced the doctrine of nonviolence. Without truth (satya) and nonviolence (ahimsa), there is nothing but the destruction of humanity. Therefore, Mahatma Gandhi emphatically stated: "The very first step in nonviolence is that we cultivate in our daily life, as between ourselves, truthfulness, humility, tolerance, loving kindness." "He also declared, "Ahimsa is the first article of my faith. It is also the last article of my creed."[42]

Social activist and Priest John Dear also praised Gandhi, saying: "In the twentieth century, Mahatma Gandhi sought this power of ahimsa at a public level in a way that no one in modern times had done."[43]

At the end of his life, the Saint of Ahimsa was overjoyed to see his country achieve independence, freedom, and democracy. However, less than a year later, on January 30, 1948, he was assassinated by a Hindu fanatic overcome by the delusion of violence (himsa), leading to his death at the age of seventy-eight.

The passing of Saint Gandhi had a profound impact worldwide. Many wept and mourned the loss of this rare "ahimsa" saint. Tenzin Gyatso, the 14th Dalai Lama,[44] visited

41 Viết Hiền, *Spring of a Saint - a Great Soul* (Mùa Xuân của một vị Thánh - một Tâm Hồn Vĩ Đại).
https://baobinhdinh.vn/562/2003/2/1967/

42 Dr. Ram Ponnu, Ahimsa: Its theory and practice in Gandhism.
https://www.mkgandhi.org/articles/ahimsa-Its-theory-and-practice-in-Gandhism.html

43 John Dear, The Experiments of Gandhi: Nonviolence In The Nuclear Age, Gandhi Journal, August, 2009.
https://www.mkgandhi.org/articles/ahimsa-Its-theory-and-practice-in-Gandhism.html

44 His Holiness the Dalai Lama, An Icon of Ahimsa - Mahatma Gandhi (1869–1948).
Published by India Today on August 21, 2021
https://www.dalailama.com/messages/transcripts-and-interviews/an-icon-

Saint Gandhi's memorial and offered his condolences:

"To me, Mahatma Gandhi represents nonviolence (Ahimsa) and compassion (Karuna). One of my main commitments today is to promote these two principles, and I believe that India is the only country capable of combining ancient knowledge with modern education. Saint Gandhi (Gandhiji) exemplifies both Ahimsa and Karuna, and I consider him a teacher of mine."

During my first visit to India in 1956, I made a pilgrimage to Rajghat on the banks of the Yamuna River, where Mahatma Gandhi was cremated. As I stood there praying, I felt very sad that I never had the chance to meet him personally, but I was also immensely inspired by the shining example of his life. To me, he was a model politician, someone who placed altruism above individual concerns and always maintained respect for all the great spiritual traditions.

---

ofahimsa-mahatma-gandhi-1869-1948

Saint Gandhi was the greatest person of our time, someone who continued until the end of his life to uphold the spirit of India and humanity as a whole. He truly believed in peace and harmony. He inspired people in Africa and America, such as Nelson Mandela and Martin Luther King Jr. Today, in a world where bullying and killing still occur, we need compassion and nonviolence more than ever. I am firmly committed to integrating these ideals with the best modern education."

4.2. DR. BHIMRAO RAMJI AMBEDKAR (1891-1956)

Professor Dr. Bhimrao Ramji Ambedkar, also known as Babasaheb Ambedkar, was a jurist and a torchbearer of Buddhist principles. He was a great beacon of equality and non-harming (ahimsa) in India in the twentieth century.

Buddhist Ambedkar Photo: Buddhist Ambedkar and the first constitution of India. (Image: Internet)

Bhimrao Ramji Ambedkar was born into a poor Dalit family in Madhya Pradesh, India. Due to his intelligence, he received support from the Maharaja of Baroda for his education expenses.

However, Indian society at the time was deeply divided into four caste groups: brahmins (priests), kshatriyas (warriors and rulers), vaishyas (merchants), and shudras (laborers and the lowest caste, often considered untouchables),[45] which subjected him to discrimination and humiliation:

> He was not allowed to sit with wealthy students.
>
> He could not play with upper-class children during recess.
>
> He was prohibited from learning Sanskrit, the sacred language of Hindu philosophy.
>
> Teachers refused to check the homework of lower-caste students.

Despite these challenges, his determination to pursue education for social reform led him to graduate with degrees in Political Science and Economics in Bombay. He then pursued a Doctorate in Economics at Columbia University and continued his studies in Economics and Political Science at the London School of Economics.

Upon returning to India, he was deeply distressed to witness the discrimination faced by lower-caste individuals, who were barred from Hindu temples and public water sources. Dr. Ambedkar then emerged as a leader in nonviolent resistance (ahimsa), advocating fiercely for justice and equality for the oppressed, inspired by the teachings of the Buddha: "In the droplet of tears and salt, there is no caste; in the droplet of blood and red, there is none" (Không có giai cấp trong giọt nước mắt cùng mặn, cũng không có giai cấp trong giọt máu cùng đỏ.)[46]

---

45 There were four classes in the caste system: Brahmins (priests and scholars), Kshatriyas (kings, governors, and warriors), Vaishyas (cattle herders, agriculturists, artisans, and merchants), and Shudras (laborers and service providers).
https://www.worldhistory.org/article/1152/caste-system-in-ancient-india/

46 Quotation in Thich Duc Truong, *The Message of Vesak* in April (Thông điệp tháng Tư).

Professor B.R. Ambedkar was appointed by Prime Minister Nehru as the Minister of Law with the responsibility of drafting India's first constitution following the country's independence from British colonial rule. Ambedkar introduced provisions promoting equality and ahimsa (non-harming) into the Indian constitution, including:

> Prohibition of all forms of discrimination between different classes of citizens.
>
> Equality for Dalits (lower caste people) and equality for women.
>
> Freedom of religion.
>
> Enhancement of the role of women in society.
>
> Support for the poor and assistance for their children's education.
>
> Equal opportunity for all to seek employment according to their abilities, without consideration of their previous caste status."[47]

B.R. Ambedkar recognized the appearance of Buddha in India amidst dissatisfaction with the caste system and deep-rooted social discrimination. He initiated a social revolution advocating for "equality" and "nonviolence" (ahimsa). Ambedkar, originally a follower of Hinduism, found the noble teachings of Buddhism compelling and formally converted, embracing its expanded path:

> Equality for all social classes.
>
> Rejection of all forms of discrimination.

---

https://phatgiao.vn/bai-viet/thong-diep-thang-tu.html
https://thuvienhoasen.org/a37411/mau-ai-cung-do-nuoc-mat-ai-cung-man-

47 A*mbedkar – The Person rekindled the Light of Buddhism* (Ambedkar - Người thắp sáng lại ngọn lửa Phật pháp)
Theo phatphap.org.vn
https://fos.ussh.vnu.edu.vn/vi/news/tan-man-phuong-dong/ambedkar-nguoi-thap-sang-lai-ngon-lua-phat-phap-150.html

Gender equality.

Freedom and democracy.

Universal access to spiritual practice and enlightenment.

Social status is determined by actions and character, not imposed societal prejudices.

Sangha as a form of democracy, welcoming all social classes.

On October 3, 1954, in a BBC broadcast, B.R. Ambedkar stated:

> My social philosophy may be said to be enshrined in three words: liberty, equality, and fraternity. I have derived them from the teachings of my master, the Buddha.
>
> I prefer Buddhism because this religion presents three combined principles that no other religion offers. All other religions are troubled with 'God,' 'soul,' and 'afterlife.' Buddhism teaches 'wisdom' (prajna), 'compassion' (karuna), and 'equality.' This is what appeals to me. These three principles can also appeal to the world. No deity or soul can save society, and only one person has spoken out against inequality and liberated the lower class, that is, Buddha.[48]

Professor B.R. Ambedkar called upon the Dalits to follow the Triple Gem (Buddha, Dharma, Sangha) because it is the path of equality, and nonviolence, and can bring happiness and liberation from the oppressive caste system. Responding to this call, on October 14, 1956, 500,000 Dalits collectively converted

48 Ravi Shankar Sing, The influence of B.R.Ambedkar's Buddhist revival movement on the socio-economic development of the untouchables in India (Ảnh hưởng của phong trào phục hưng Phật giáo của B.R.Ambedkar vào việc phát triển kinh tế-xã hội của tầng lớp tiện dân ở Ấn Độ). http://hoangphap.info/Page.aspx?ArticleID=6081&SubID=5&ID=6

to the Triple Gem. Indeed, this was a historic day that marked the revival of Buddhism in India."[49]

Dr. Babasaheb Ambedkar's nonviolence was the spiritual strength of an individual who used ideas, reasoning, and gentle persuasion to oppose the ancient injustices of Indian society and awaken the community. This approach succeeded in inspiring 500,000 Dalits to commit to the path of nonviolence and embrace Buddhism. The concept of nonviolence, enshrined in the first constitution of an independent India, continues to guide the Indian people towards peaceful and happy living to this day.

Dr. Ambedkar and his wife and 500,000 untouchables are taking refuge in the Three Jewels. (Image: Internet)

49 Ambedkar – the Person rekindled the Light of Buddhism (Ambedkar - Người thắp sáng lại ngọn lửa Phật pháp)
Theo phatphap.org.vn
https://fos.ussh.vnu.edu.vn/vi/news/tan-man-phuong-dong/ambedkar-nguoi-thap-sang-lai-ngon-lua-phat-phap-150.html

It's unfortunate that shortly after, within less than two months, Dr. Babasaheb Ambedkar passed away. His contributions "Babasaheb"[50] as a dedicated Buddhist monk, a brilliant legal scholar, the first Law Minister of independent India, and a social reformer advocating equality and nonviolence (ahimsa) have been recognized by the nation of India. The Ambedkar National Memorial was established in New Delhi, where Dr. Ambedkar passed away on December 6, 1956, and his birthday is commemorated across India.

4.3. BODHISATTVA THICH QUANG DUC (1897-1963)

The nonviolent struggle methods of Mahatma Gandhi and Dr. Bhimrao Ramji Ambedkar had a direct and strong impact on the movement against religious discrimination by the Southern Vietnamese Buddhist community under the government of Ngo Dinh Diem in 1963.

In India, Mahatma Gandhi called upon Indians to rise for independence from British rule in the spirit of nonviolence (ahimsa), while Dr. Bhimrao Ramji Ambedkar led the lower caste conversion movement, relying on the Triple Gem to peacefully fight (ahimsa) for equality amidst caste discrimination. Similarly, in Vietnam, there was Bodhisattva Thich Quang Duc (1897-1963), self-immolated to protest and fight for religious equality under the regime of Ngo Dinh Diem in South Saigon.

Venerable Thich Quang Duc, born Lâm Văn Tuất in 1897 in Khanh Hoa province, entered monastic life at the age of 7 and received full ordination at 20. He contributed to the construction and renovation of 14 temples in Central Vietnam. In 1943, he

50 Babasaheb: Father, Nhà Sáng Lập.
Babasaheb (Devanagari: बाबासाहेब, IAST: Bābāsāhēb) is a nickname given in India. It is a Marathi phrase which means "Respected Father" (Baba = father and Saheb = sir).
https://www.google.com/search?q=babasaheb

moved to South Vietnam to propagate Buddhism and served as Deputy Superior at Xa Loi Pagoda, Saigon. On June 11, 1963, he self-immolated to advocate for religious equality. He lived to the age of 66, with 46 years in the monkhood.

President Ngo Dinh Diem (a devout Catholic) aimed to eliminate Buddhism from the spiritual and religious life of the people of South Vietnam. He allowed only the national flag to be displayed, excluding the Buddhist flag, intending to diminish the influence of Buddhism across society. On January 9, 1956, Diem issued Decree No. 4, abolishing Buddha's birthday as a public holiday for civil servants and soldiers, and prohibiting the display of the Buddhist flag on Vesak Day.

In early May 1963, in the South, hanging flags on Vesak Day was banned. Eight Buddhists protested at the Hue radio station, where they were massacred, and many Buddhist people were arrested, beaten, and kidnapped, temples were sealed off, and religious freedom was violated. Confronted with such brutal oppression by Diem's government, monks, and Buddhists, from rural areas to urban areas, united in opposing the repression of Buddhism and struggling against the authoritarian regime, family rule, and the religious tyranny of the dictatorship. On May 7, 1963, Southern Vietnamese Buddhists decided to publicly announce their forms of struggle with basic strategies as follows:

Nature: Purely religious

Objective: Fight for human rights, religious equality, and freedom of Buddhist beliefs

Option 1: Speak out, intervene, persuade, negotiate peacefully

Option 2: Buddhist monks and followers protest, and march in opposition

Option 3: Nonviolent fasting (ahimsa)

Option 4: The peak of conflict: Self-immolation is the

highest form, and self-sacrifice is the highest of nonviolence.

To warn the Diem regime against exceeding its authority over religious freedoms and favoring one religion over another, Buddhism proposed five reasonable and feasible requests. However, the Diem government showed no willingness to resolve the issues, ignoring and allowing the Saigon military to continue directly imprisoning, beating, oppressing, and kidnapping innocent monks, Buddhists, students, and civilians.

The peak of conflict and discord arrived at the end of May 1963. Venerable Thich Quang Duc wrote a letter requesting permission for self-immolation, which was initially rejected by Buddhist leaders. By early June, with the crisis seemingly deadlocked and unable to tolerate such rampant abuse of power, Buddhism agreed to elevate its nonviolent struggle to its highest form—a form full of compassion, empathy, and sacrifice. They allowed Bodhisattva Thich Quang Duc to self-immolate, burning his body as a dramatic protest against the oppressive regime of Diem, hoping to awaken and stir the leadership of the government.

In his gentle and awakening letter to President Diem before self-immolation, devoid of any hatred or resentment, chief monk Venerable Quang Duc wrote with a deep concern for the path his nation was taking:

"I pray that the Buddha will support President Ngo Dinh Diem to wisely accept the five minimal requests of Vietnamese Buddhism... I pray for peace in the country and the happiness of the people..."[51]

This act was a poignant moment in history, symbolizing a profound commitment to principles of nonviolence and a plea

51 Unknown author. The letter "Heartfelt prayer" of Bodhisattva Thich Quang Duc before self-immolation
(Bức thư "Lời nguyện tâm huyết" của Bồ Tát Thich Quang Duc trước khi tự thiêu).
https://quangduc.com/a6759/buc-thu-loi-nguyen-tam-huyet-cua-bo-tat-thich-quang-duc-truoc-khi-tu-thieu

for justice and religious freedom.

The historic moment of June 11, 1963, had arrived, witnessed by the world as more than 800 monks marched. Then, precisely at 9:17 a.m., chief Monk Thích Quang Duc peacefully sat in meditation, striking a match and self-immolating at the intersection of Le Van Duyet and Phan Dinh Phung in Saigon, in the presence of police forces, Buddhists, and foreign journalists.

The nonviolent struggle spirit of Bodhisattva Thich Quang Duc, and the fierce fervor of the Buddhist monks and followers, were intense. They resolutely protected Bodhisattva Thich Quang Duc by encircling him in multiple rings. Many lay down in front of fire trucks, and police vehicles, enduring beatings from police batons, to obstruct any attempts to disrupt this sacred moment of self-sacrifice, this extraordinary moment of nonviolence (ahimsa) by Bodhisattva Thich Quang Duc.

Bodhisattva Thich Quang Duc
in the flames of self-immolation. (Image: Malcolm Browne)

Oh, a heroic flame blazing brightly! Yet, his relic heart remained intact, as if to leave behind a message of love for humanity and Vietnamese Buddhism. His immense and noble vow of nonviolence (ahimsa) radiated so profoundly that his heart turned into a diamond, unscathed by the heat of the flames. The powerful essence of his compassion and extraordinary wisdom forged this transcendent heart.

Heart of Bodhisattva Thich Quang Duc
intact, immortal, unburnt. (Image: Malcolm Browne)

A sacred and divine heart amidst ordinary life! A noble, courageous, and heroic death for the faith! Millions of hearts around the world shed tears and bowed in awe, moved by the nonviolent struggle and great sacrifice of Bodhisattva Thich Quang Duc.

The world revered him, and nearly all media outlets everywhere republished this powerful and poignant image of self-immolation. As Professor Tran Van Giau noted: "The extraordinary and brave sacrifice of Venerable Thich Quang Duc, his image sitting upright like a stone statue in the blazing flames, spread quickly like an electric wave, stirring public opinion throughout Vietnam and the world."[52]

On June 14, the New York Times headlined, "U.S. Warns

South Vietnam on Demands of Buddhists: Diem is told he faces censure if he fails to satisfy religious grievances, many of which are called just." Historian Seth Jacobs remarked that Venerable Thich Quang Duc "also reduced America's Diem experiment to ashes."

Indeed, although nonviolent and peaceful, not cause bloodshed or injury, the spiritual strength of Thich Quang Duc's nonviolent act was a turning point that shook an entire regime and awakened a world full of violence and injustice. As a result, in early November 1963, the pivotal moment led to the overthrow of the U.S.-backed Ngo Dinh Diem regime.

In September 2010, a memorial monument for Bodhisattva Thich Quang Duc was inaugurated in Saigon, at the very location where he self-immolated. Every year, both in Vietnam and abroad, ceremonies are held to commemorate the martyrdom of Bodhisattva Thich Quang Duc.

Memorial monument of
Bodhisattva Thich Quang Duc. (Image: Giác Ngộ Online)

52 *Trần Văn Giàu, The South kept its Citadel* (Miền Nam giữ vững thành đồng), Vol II. Publishing Khoa học, Hà Nội, 1966, tr. 342. https://thuvienhoasen.org/a13472/suc-manh-bat-bao-dong-nhin-tu-ngon-lua-thich-quang-duc-le-cung

4.4. MARTIN LUTHER KING JR. (1929-1968)

In the mid-twentieth century, the world witnessed many famous nonviolent struggles (ahimsa), such as Mahatma Gandhi (India) against British colonial rule, Dr. Bhimrao Ramji Ambedkar (India) fighting caste discrimination, and Bodhisattva Thich Quang Duc (Vietnam) whose self-immolation highlighted the oppression of Buddhism by the Ngo Dinh Diem regime. These indomitable images, to varying degrees, inspired Dr. Martin Luther King Jr. in leading the civil rights movement, aiming to end racial discrimination and violence in the United States.

Reverend Martin Luther King Jr., a Southern Baptist, was an African American born in 1929 in Atlanta, Georgia, into a middle-class family with three generations of ministers. In 1955, he earned a Ph.D. in Theology and was gifted in public speaking. He was a human rights activist, laying the foundation for racial equality, had a significant impact on American history, and won the Nobel Peace Prize.

In modern history, starting from the 17th century, African Americans crossed the Atlantic Ocean to live in America as slaves to white masters. The Civil War (1860-1865) over the issue of slavery took place between the Union (the North) and the Confederacy (the South). In 1863, President Lincoln, leading the Union, issued the "Emancipation Proclamation" law.

However, in the twentieth century, colored people were still discriminated against, similar to the lower castes in India, meaning they would "dirty" buses, roads, restaurants, and restrooms by using them alongside white people. Thus, colored people were prohibited from using public facilities with whites, such as buses, trains, restaurants, and restrooms. If they encountered whites, they had to give up their seats, sit at the back, and use facilities designated for colored people. They were often scorned, beaten, humiliated, bullied, and murdered.

It began in late 1955 when a colored worker named Rosa

Parks refused to stand up and give her seat to a white person on a bus in Montgomery, Alabama. This sparked numerous protests demanding justice and equal rights for African Americans in the southern United States.

The Ku Klux Klan, an extremist white supremacist group often protected by local police, perpetrated many violent acts against colored people, such as burning cars, and churches, and senselessly beating, harassing, and killing them.

In the 1950s, the young pastor Martin Luther King Jr. began tirelessly advocating for the civil rights of colored people through nonviolent struggle (ahimsa). Because of this, he became a prominent leader in the fight for equality in America despite facing many challenges, including imprisonment, surveillance, harassment, bombings, and ultimately being assassinated by a "violent fanatic" in 1968 at the young age of 38.

The notable contributions of Martin Luther King Jr. in using nonviolence (ahimsa) to combat racial discrimination are known as follows:

Martin Luther King Jr. organized the protest and boycott of the Montgomery public buses in Alabama, which lasted for over a year. Despite being arrested, he remained steadfast in his pursuit of equality for African Americans and minorities, stating, "Our capacity to endure will wear you down."[53]

On August 28, 1963, Martin Luther King Jr. led a peaceful march in the nation's capital, Washington D.C., where he delivered his iconic and stirring speech "I Have a Dream" in front of more than 250,000 participants at the Lincoln Memorial. The speech articulated a vision of a world where people are judged not by the color of their skin but by the content of their character. This idea resonates with the teachings of the Buddha, who taught that one's worth is not determined by social class or skin color, but by

53 "I Have a Dream" Speech by Dr. Martin Luther King, Jr. March on Washington for Jobs and Freedom, August 28, 1963. https://www.marshall.edu/onemarshallu/i-have-a-dream/

actions, deeds, and character. King famously declared, "We are all equal, there are no classes in the blood and the tears. Whose blood is also red and whose tears are also salty."[54]

Pastor Martin Luther King, Jr.
speaking "I Have a Dream." (Image: Internet)

This groundbreaking speech is considered one of the greatest in U.S. history, raising public awareness of the civil

54 As previously mentioned in section 2.9. Buddha used equality and non-harming (ahimsa) to revolutionize society.
Minh Duc Trieu Tam Anh, A lowly caste girl felt in love Venerable Ānanda (Cô Gái Hạ Tiện Yêu Tôn Giả Ānanda): One Life, One Sun and Moon (Một cuộc đời, Một vầng nhật nguyệt). Episode 6. Publishing House: Văn Học. 2014.
https://thuvienhoasen.org/a21264/co-gai-ha-tien-yeu-ton-gia-nanda

rights movement, and promoting reform, and societal change. As a resounding outcome, on July 2, 1964, President Lyndon B. Johnson signed into law the Civil Rights Act, officially recognizing freedom and equality as fundamental rights protected by law.

The civil rights organization for African Americans was founded by Reverend Martin Luther King Jr., the Southern Christian Leadership Conference (SCLC), where he also served as its first president.

He applied pressure to abolish Jim Crow laws (a series of racial segregation laws) through nonviolent sit-ins and peaceful marches, compelling businesses and public places to serve African American customers.

Luther King played a crucial role in the passage of the Civil Rights Act of 1964 and the Voting Rights Act of 1965, aimed at ending racial segregation and discriminatory practices in the country.

Luther King led hundreds of thousands of Americans in protests to improve economic and social conditions for the impoverished and opposed the Vietnam War.

With his eloquence and passionate heart, Martin Luther King Jr. delivered over 2,500 speeches, wrote numerous articles, and published five books between 1957 and 1968 to inspire equality and call for the elimination of racial discrimination.

Martin Luther King's influence through nonviolence (ahimsa) in his efforts to build peace and justice not only impacted Americans but also spread worldwide. In 1964, at the age of 35, Martin Luther King became the youngest recipient of the Nobel Peace Prize.

Statues of Reverend Martin Luther King Jr. have been erected in many places across the United States. His birthday is celebrated as an official holiday in the U.S., and his name has been given to roads not only in America[55] but also in Vietnam[56] and many other places around the world.

Statue of black civil rights activist Martin Luther King, Jr. on the National Mall, Washington D.C. (Image: Internet)

55 For example: There is Martin Luther King Blvd, Riverside, California.
56 Luther King Avenue. Phú Mỹ Hưng Town, the 7 District, HCM City, VN.

CHAPTER 5

CONCLUSION

In this article, the spirit of Ahimsa of Lord Buddha, Emperor Aśoka of ancient times, as well as Mahatma Gandhi, Dr. Bhimrao Ramji Ambedkar, Bodhisattva Thich Quang Duc, and Martin Luther King Jr. in modern times have been introduced.

5.1. THE PEACE ACTIVISTS' DECLARATION OF NONVIOLENCE

Declarations on Nonviolence by Peace Activists The declarations of peace, equality, and nonviolence (ahimsa) by these six social revolutionaries have had significant impact, as follows:

"There is no caste in tears, they are all salty; there is no caste in blood, it is all red. Lord Buddha."[57] (The Buddha)

"Following the path of nonviolence (ahimsa) has a yardstick. But we cannot follow that path of peace if we remain enslaved to vices like jealousy, impatience, cruelty, hastiness, superficiality,

57 Quotation in Thich Duc Truong, *The Message of Vesak* in April (Thông điệp tháng Tư).
https://phatgiao.vn/bai-viet/thong-diep-thang-tu.html
https://thuvienhoasen.org/a37411/mau-ai-cung-do-nuoc-mat-ai-cung-man-

laziness, and passivity."[58] (King Aśoka)

"Without truth and nonviolence (ahimsa), there is nothing but destruction for humanity."[59](Mahatma Gandhi)

"Implementing policies of equality and nonviolence towards religion to uphold the eternal nation."[60] (Bodhisattva Thich Quang Duc)

"Violence brings only temporary victories; violence, by creating more social problems than it solves, never brings permanent peace."[61](Martin Luther King Jr)

5.2. SOLUTION OF NONVIOLENCE AGAINST

58 K. R. Norman, Buddhism and Aśoka King 9 Phật Giáo và A-dục Vương). Collection of articles about King Aśoka and Vietnamese trans by Nguyên Tâm. https://quangduc.com/a27861/Aśoka-cuoc-doi-va-su-nghiep-tuyen-tap-cac-bai-viet-ve-vua-a-duc

59 Dr. Ram Ponnu. Ahimsa: *Its Theory and Practice in Gandhism.* https://www.mkgandhi.org/articles/ahimsa-Its-theory-and-practice-in-Gandhism.html

60 Quotation in Châu Thành, *Bodhisattva Thich Quang Duc his Will to Heart* (Bồ Tát Thich Quang Duc Từ Lời Nguyện Đến Trái Tim) https://thuvienhoasen.org/a17333/bo-tat-thich-quang-duc-tu-loi-nguyen-den-trai-tim

61 80 Martin Luther King Jr. Quotes that inspire courage, peace, and justice (80 Câu Trích Dẫn Của Martin Luther King Jr Truyền Cảm Hứng Về Lòng Dũng Cảm, Hòa Bình Và Sự Công Bằng). Collected by Hoàng Thị Thùy Dung. https://ivolunteervietnam.com/80-cau-trich-dan-cua-martin-luther-king-jr-truyen-cam-hung-ve-long-dung-cam-hoa-binh-va-su-cong-bang.html

OPPRESSION, RACIAL DISCRIMINATION

The common solution of six peace activists and leaders of many movements against war, advocating for peace and racial discrimination, is as follows:

1. Transformation of the Conflict

Call for and inspire the public to recognize the value of ahimsa and civil rights (the right to equality and justice), break the chains of oppression, injustice, discrimination, and classism.

Negotiate peacefully according to the needs of all parties involved (win the heart).

Place high value on choosing ahimsa as the primary option to avoid conflict and war.

2. Application of Ahimsa

Resolve strategic resistance conflicts through methods such as psychological, political, or economic pressure to bring about societal change, including marches, strikes, civil disobedience, boycotts, and non-cooperation.

Refrain from livelihoods involving manufacturing, production, or trade of toxic substances, weapons (nuclear, biological, firearms, etc.) that lead to violence and human destruction.

Abandon violent killing (ahimsa), violence, and war.

Advocate for abolishing the death penalty (violent killing), replacing it with life imprisonment, education, rehabilitation (according to statistics62 from 195 UN member states, 55 countries still maintain the death

62 *Death Penalty by Country and Territory* (Tử hình theo quốc gia và vùng lãnh thổ).
https://vi.wikipedia.org/wiki/

penalty).

Be proactive, dynamic, and maintain nonviolent resistance strategies until success is achieved.

Develop compassion and understanding to transform hatred, war, and conflict into expansive love, recognizing that we are all human beings sharing one planet.

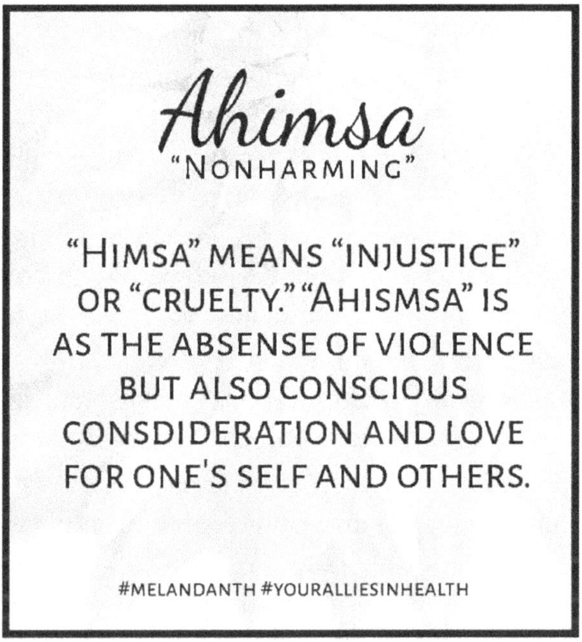

5.3. CONTRIBUTIONS OF BUDDHISM TO PEACEFUL LIVING AND NONVIOLENCE

Buddhism has contributed to a peaceful way of life, free from war, killing, and hatred. Nonviolence (ahimsa) forms the foundation for global peace-building. The methods and principles of social change by Lord Buddha and ancient King Aśoka can be seen as ahead of their time and pioneering for later nonviolent revolutionary movements in modern times, such as those led by Mahatma Gandhi, Dr. Bhimrao Ramji Ambedkar,

Bodhisattva Thich Quang Duc, Martin Luther King, Jr., and others.

These revolutionaries have contributed to societal change, the struggle for civil rights, and the liberation of humanity from racial discrimination, oppression, slavery, and violence. Due to their practice of non-harm (ahimsa), they are honored as saints, bodhisattvas, enlightened beings, and great heroes of nonviolence (without carrying firearms). Therefore, the principle of "nonviolence" (ahimsa), akin to a golden rule, holds particular value in promoting principles of freedom, equality, and inspiration not only in India, Vietnam, and the United States but also globally, as dreamed by Martin Luther King Jr.:

"I have a dream that one day my four little children will live in a nation where they will not be judged by the color of their skin but by the content of their character."[63]

Currently, many countries and individuals are competing to possess advanced violent weapons such as nuclear weapons, biological weapons, bacterial weapons, and firearms. This is truly dangerous.

Humanity is witnessing various types of conflicts at different levels, from personal to national to global. Severe conflicts, disagreements, and wars on many fronts (religious, political, economic, educational, and emotional) are accompanied by violent weapons of modern nations, both developed and developing. This can lead to wars, suicide bombings, and social violence erupting at any time, resulting in countless innocent civilians, soldiers, and religious followers losing their lives, as seen in bloody conflicts like Russia-Ukraine, Israel-Hamas, the Houthi civil war (Yemen), Myanmar, Pakistan, Afghanistan, Syria, and more. The United Nations and many countries

63 "I Have a Dream" Speech by the Rev. Martin Luther King Jr. at the "March on Washington," 1963 (excerpts)
https://www.gilderlehrman.org/sites/default/files/inline-pdfs/king.dreamspeech.excerpts.pdf

around the world call for peaceful solutions and ceasefires, but they have yet to be effective. Therefore, the virtue of ahimsa is always necessary to spread, educate, and inspire everyone, holding enduring value for future generations as well.

Beyond bringing about a peaceful, stable, and just society, ahimsa holds significant value in spiritual life. The Buddha recognized ahimsa as a fundamental precept for anyone aspiring to ascend the path of sages, liberate themselves from the cycle of birth and death, attain enlightenment, and become a Buddha. This is the path of moral conduct (śīla), which leads to concentration (samādhi) and wisdom (prajñā). Śīla-samādhi-prajñā, the threefold training, aids in achieving complete liberation and becoming a saint filled with compassion in this world. Therefore, Dr. K. N. Jayatilleke[64] also affirmed:

"It is through compassion and nonviolence (ahimsa) that Buddhism has spread across a vast region of Asia peacefully, without any interference from force or political power. Not a single drop of blood has been shed in propagating the Dharma; no killings have occurred in the name of Buddhism or the Buddha. This is indeed a source of great pride!"

Society would be beautiful if one person practiced ahimsa (non-harming), and even more so if many families and communities practiced ahimsa, as conflicts, disagreements, and wars would cease. Consequently, the cycle of birth and death would also be liberated. As the ancients taught:

If all beings refrain from killing,

The world would have no wars.

Every home and every place practiced virtue,

Why worry that the world won't be at peace!

Indeed, Buddhism has greatly contributed to leading

64 Thích Trí Giải, *The Nature of Violence Between Religions and the Nonviolent Spirit of Buddhism* (Tính Chất Bạo Động Giữa Các Tôn Giáo và Tinh Thần Bất Bạo Động Của Phật Giáo). http://www.phatgiaodaichung.com/Bai2011_04/002batbaodong.htm

humanity toward a way of life that is peaceful, happy, equal, and free from violent conflicts, wars, and hatred.

5.4. BUDDHISM IS CONSIDERED AS THE FUTURE RELIGION, THE GLOBAL RELIGION

Despite 2,600 years passing, the teachings of the Buddha still exist and have developed all over the world. The Buddha Shakyamuni is rightfully considered the greatest figure among all the great figures in the world, as the renowned mathematician and physicist Albert Einstein honored him, saying:

"The religion of the future will be a cosmic religion. It should transcend a personal god and avoid dogmas and theology. Covering both the natural and the spiritual, it should be based on a religious sense arising from the experience of all things, natural and spiritual, as a meaningful unity. Buddhism answers this description."[65]

Buddhism stands out as a religion that meets these conditions, embracing both the natural and the supernatural, and founded on a sense of morality derived from comprehensive experience. Therefore, Buddhism is poised to be the religion of the future, resonating with global unity and timeless wisdom.

65 Thích Nguyên Tạng, *Scientist Albert Einstein and Buddhism* (Nhà Khoa Học Albert Einstein và Đạo Phật). https://www.buddhismtoday.com/viet/pgtg/nguoi/013-albert.htm

APPENDIX

The owners of website thuvienhoasen.org[66] would like to introduce: Buddhism, the religion of compassion and wisdom, always respects and values the lives of all sentient beings.

The Buddha appeared in this world intending to bring peace and happiness to both devas and humans. Indeed, from ancient times to the present, Buddhism has never brought suffering to anyone. Buddhism only offers a path to transform suffering for those who seek to understand and aspire to follow it.

This is the introduction by Ven. Dr. Bhikṣuṇī Gioi Huong at the seminar on "Buddhist Views on the Death Penalty" at Phuoc Hau Temple in Milwaukee on October 28, 2006. Readers are invited to continue with the presentation by the nun:

THE FUNDAMENTAL TEACHINGS OF THE BUDDHA ON THE DEATH PENALTY

Ven. Dr. Bhikṣuṇī Gioi Huong

Buddhism, the religion of compassion and wisdom, always respects and values the lives of all sentient beings. The Buddha appeared in this world intending to bring peace and happiness to both devas and humans. Indeed, from ancient times to the present, Buddhism has never brought suffering to anyone.

66 https://thuvienhoasen.org/a4160/xin-cho-biet-quan-diem-cua-phat-giao-ve-hinh-phat-an-tu-hinh

Buddhism only offers a path to transform suffering for those who seek to understand and aspire to follow it.

Illustration of the death penalty in Vietnam during the French colonial period. (Image: Internet)

Today, on the occasion of the Milwaukee City Friendship Association's talk on the Buddhist perspective on the death penalty, we will clarify this topic with the following ideas:

I. The Five Precepts

The important and fundamental precepts guiding spiritual development that are very familiar to Buddhists are the observance of the Five Precepts (Panca Sila)[1]:

1. I undertake the precept to refrain from killing any living being.
2. I undertake the precept to refrain from taking what is not given.
3. I undertake the precept to refrain from sexual misconduct.
4. I undertake the precept to refrain from false speech.

5. I undertake the precept to refrain from intoxicating drinks and drugs that lead to carelessness.

In their negative aspect, these precepts are prohibitions, meaning that one should not commit any sins or crimes. The nature of these prohibitions is manifested in two aspects:

(a) to prevent and guard against sins or crimes, such as prohibiting the consumption of alcohol as it may lead to committing sins or crimes;

(b) to stop and not repeat any committed crimes, such as killing, stealing, sexual misconduct, lying, etc., which are inherently unwholesome.

In their positive aspect, the first precept helps us cultivate compassion. The second precept can help nurture honesty and a generous spirit, free from attachment and right livelihood. The third precept helps cultivate self-restraint, protecting the senses and emotions, and controlling worldly desires. The fourth precept fosters trust, truthfulness, and moral integrity. The final precept helps us return to mindfulness, awareness, and wisdom.

Therefore, diligently practicing the Buddhist precepts will help us live a moral life, enhance spiritual life on an individual level, and at the same time promote peaceful coexistence based on cooperation and trust in the community, thereby advancing social progress.

II. The First Precept

The first precept supports the inclination to oppose the destruction of life. This is based on the principle of a benevolent mind and the respect for the right to life of all beings.

In the Brahmajala Sūtra[2], the Buddha detailed the first Bodhisattva precept as follows: "A disciple of the Buddha must not kill, cause others to kill, encourage others to kill, praise killing, rejoice in seeing killing, use spells to kill, or even provide the means for killing. They should not act as an agent or participate in killing through various means."

There are five conditions[3] that constitute the act of killing:

1. There is a living being, whether human or animal.
2. Recognizing that this being is alive.
3. Intending or deciding to kill.
4. Employing appropriate means to carry out the act of killing.
5. A resulting death occurs.

If any of these conditions are missing, the act of killing is not complete, even if death occurs. It is then considered an accident and does not incur the sin of killing the person who committed the act.

There are six ways of killing[4]: (1) killing with one's own hand, (2) ordering others to kill, (3) killing by shooting, throwing stones, hitting with sticks, etc., (4) killing by setting traps, (5) killing by using supernatural powers or mysterious methods, and (6) killing by using spells or occult science.

No matter which means is used to kill or destroy the spiritual life of a being, the person committing the act incurs the karma of killing.

Therefore, a true Buddhist cannot carry out or support the death penalty because the death penalty equates to taking or ending a human life with the five conditions and any of the six methods mentioned above.

III. The Heart of Compassion

In the first precept of the Brahmajala Sūtra[5], the Buddha teaches that "a Buddhist ought to always have compassion, filial piety, and should strive to save all beings. However, if a person recklessly takes life, they have committed a grave offense against the Bodhisattva precepts."

By adhering to this precept, we learn to cultivate both loving-kindness (metta) and compassion (karuna). We should love others as ourselves. By feeling the suffering of others as our own, we will naturally seek ways to alleviate their pain.

Thus, we develop compassion and grow in altruism for the benefit of others, fostering an awareness of respect and protection for all beings.

In the Metta Sutta (Loving-kindness Sutta), the Buddha also teaches:

May all beings be happy;
May they be joyous and live in safety.
All living beings,
Whether weak or strong,
In high,middle or low realms of existence,
Small or great, visible or invisible,
Near or far, born or to be born,
May all beings be happy.
Let none deceive another,
Nor despise any being in any state.
Let none through anger or ill-will
Wish harm upon another.
Even as a mother protects her life Her child, her only child,
So with a boundless heart
Should one cherish all living beings,
Radiating kindness over the entire world[6].

IV. Buddha Nature

Another reason why Buddhism does not support capital punishment is that the Buddha taught that the intrinsic nature of all beings (humans or animals) is pure; more specifically, it is the pure mind, whose ultimate nature is enlightenment or Buddha nature (Buddha), also known as Buddha wisdom.

As the Buddha states in the Lotus Sūtra[7], "I see that all beings possess the Buddha-nature and that they are endowed with virtues, behaving with dignity and are fundamentally pure like a precious jewel."

Therefore, if people become violent, it could be for various reasons, but one primary reason is the arising of evil thoughts, often influenced by their environment and circumstances. However, everyone has the potential to improve and return to their true, innate Buddha nature.

V. Non-Killing

As mentioned, all beings have Buddha nature. Therefore, we should not only refrain from killing people but also avoid harming animals. Moreover, in some cases, due to karmic circumstances, humans can be reborn as animals, and animals can be reborn as humans.

A fundamental guiding principle in Buddhism for cultivating virtue is non-harming (ahimsa) – the prohibition against causing injury or death to any living being.

Since we desire to live, we should not kill others, including other living beings. Furthermore, the karma of killing is considered the root of all suffering and the fundamental cause of diseases and wars, and these destructive forces are essentially aligned with demonic forces.

The ultimate and universal ideal of Buddhism is to serve tirelessly until the complete and permanent cessation of all suffering for all beings, not just humans.

As the Buddha says in the Brahmajala Sūtra[8], "Whenever a Bodhisattva[9] sees a person preparing to kill an animal, they should skillfully intervene to rescue and protect it, liberating it from its difficult and painful situation…"

VI. Vegetarianism

The expansive compassion towards all beings means not only refraining from harming humans and animals but also adhering to rules of self-preservation such as practicing vegetarianism. These are positive and authentic teachings from the Buddha related to the development of human character.

All sentient beings –
Whether human or animal,
Fear death and seek life.
They are terrified of the butcher's knife,
Chopping them into pieces.
Instead of cruelty and cowardice,
Why not cease killing and cherish life? [10]

The Buddha encourages vegetarianism as a natural and reasonable requirement consistent with the precept of non-harming. The Bodhisattva precepts explicitly prohibit the consumption of meat. The venerable Great Assembler asked the Buddha, 'Why does the Tathagata not allow the eating of meat?' The Buddha replied, 'Because eating meat cuts off the great seed of compassion.' [11] We should not limit our compassion only to favored beings or creatures, but extend it to all sentient beings, even those who may have transgressed. Compassion forms the foundation for all our interactions with others, without needing to dwell on what their views and actions are.

VII. Retribution

For certain reasons and purposes, society's legal system imposes the death penalty. This punishment is used to punish criminals, prevent them from repeating their evil actions, and serve as a warning to others. However, it is also clearly a form of revenge in a more subtle sense.

We need to reduce fear, hatred, and the desire for revenge through torture and killing.

The concept of revenge is entirely unfamiliar in Buddhism. The death penalty is the harshest form of punishment aimed at permanently ending a living life. When a prisoner is executed, there is no opportunity for them to change, rehabilitate, or make amends for the harm they caused.

Will executing someone convicted of murder bring the victim back to life?

Certainly not. So, what benefit does the death penalty have?

The Buddha taught:

"Hatred does not cease through hatred,
Only through non-hatred does it cease
This is the eternal law"[12]

VIII. Psychology

According to Buddhist teachings, the conditions for the next life (rebirth) depend on the final thoughts, specifically the last mental state of a person before death. The psyche or mental state of a criminal certainly cannot achieve a peaceful state. Forcing such a person to face execution may intensify their mental state, filled with anger and fear. Consequently, if they are reborn as a human, they may be even more violent than before. As they grow up, they might continue to commit even worse offenses than those in their previous life.

In the Discourse on the Differentiation of Karmic Retributions (Middle Length Discourses, No. 135), the Buddha says:

"Here, monks, there is a woman or man who is angry, irritable, and harbors many ill intentions. If even slightly provoked, they become displeased, and hostile, and show their anger, hatred, and discontent. Because of such karma, they experience such conditions, and such results; after the breakup of the body, they are reborn in a realm of suffering... If reborn as a human, they will bear a hideous appearance. This path leads to ugliness, which means anger, hatred, and discontent."

Therefore, we should avoid causing psychological unrest for prisoners, as they will have to confront death reluctantly and unwillingly.

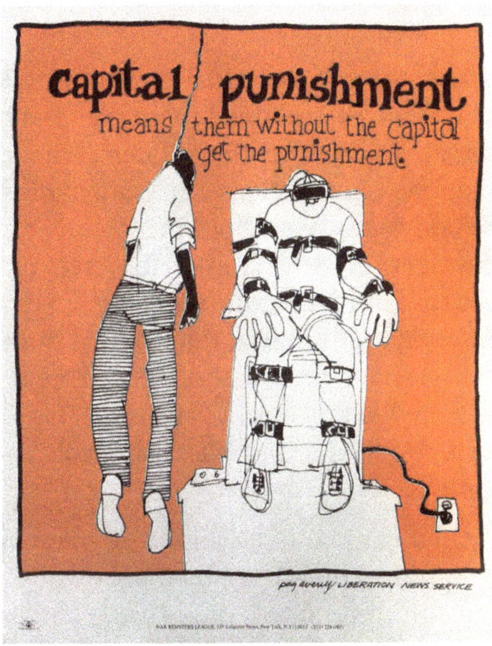

Death penalty by hanging or lethal injection. (Image: Internet)

IX. Law of Karma

Karma, or actions, are capabilities arising from the thoughts, words, and behaviors of individuals. It can be virtuous, non-virtuous, or neutral, and it deeply influences the rebirth of all sentient beings.

Non-virtuous karma leads to rebirth in one of the three lower realms (hell, hungry ghost, or animal); virtuous karma leads to rebirth as a human, a heavenly being, or a realm of formlessness. The karma of meditation and concentration leads to rebirth in the realms of form or formlessness.[14]

In the Telakatahagatha Sūtra, it states clearly: "Whoever destroys the life of any living being, in their next rebirth, that person may die suddenly at the height of their prosperity, even if they are living a comfortable, wealthy, and beautiful life..."[15]

The Buddha taught:[16]

"Here, monks, there is a woman or man who kills, is cruel, bloodstained, with a mind inclined to murder and harm, without compassion for all kinds of sentient beings. Due to such karma, they experience such conditions, and such results; after the breakup of the body, they are reborn in a realm of misery, an evil destination, torment, or hell. If after the breakup of the body, they do not get reborn in a realm of misery, an evil destination, torment, or hell, and if they are reborn as a human, wherever they are born, they will have a short life. This path leads to a short life, monks, which means killing, cruelty, bloodstains, and a mind inclined to murder and harm, without compassion for sentient beings.

But here, monks, there is a woman or man who renounces killing, abstains from killing, lays aside the stick and sword, is scrupulous and full of kindness, and lives compassionately for the welfare of all sentient beings and living beings. Due to such karma, they experience such conditions, and such results; after the breakup of the body, they are reborn in a good destination, a heavenly realm, in a fortunate existence. If after the breakup of the body, they do not get reborn in a good destination, a heavenly realm, in a fortunate existence, and if they are reborn as a human, wherever they are born, they will have a long life. This path leads to a long life, monks, which means renouncing killing, abstaining from killing, laying aside the stick and sword, being scrupulous and full of kindness, and living compassionately for the welfare of all sentient beings and living beings.

Therefore, based on the reasoning presented here, it is clear that even acts of violence, including acts of cruelty, will create negative karma for the perpetrator and diminish the possibility of a peaceful death for them.

X. Buddhist Scriptures

The rejection of the death penalty is a topic often mentioned in Buddhism, which we can see implied through the verses of the Buddha presented in the scriptures and treatises of both the Primitive Buddhism and Mahayana traditions (here I will mention a few representative cases) as follows:

A. Primitive Buddhism

1. Dhammapada:

- Verse 129: "Everyone fears punishment,

  Everyone fears death.

  Comparing others to oneself,

  One should neither kill nor cause others to kill."[17]

- Verse 130: "Everyone fears punishment,

  Everyone loves life.

  Comparing others to oneself,

  One should neither kill nor cause others to kill."[18]

- Verse 391: "Renouncing violence toward all living beings,

  Weak or strong, timid or bold,

  One should neither kill nor cause others to kill,

  This is called a 'Brahmin."[19]

2. Jataka Talcs:

i. Previous Lives of the Buddha (Deer King Banian)

In the Jataka [20], it is recounted that in a previous life, the Buddha was born as a deer king named Nyagrodha. He willingly sacrificed his own life to save a pregnant doe from being sacrificed to a king. In another past life, the Buddha sacrificed his life to provide food for a hungry tiger and its two cubs trapped in the snow.

He believed that saving lives is more meaningful than merely protecting one's self. He considered it better to lose his own life than to harm other sentient beings.

There are many stories from the Buddha's past lives as a bodhisattva where he observed the precept of nonviolence, sacrificed his life to uphold moral integrity, and nurtured compassion.

The Buddha said:

> Moreover, I have observed thus: "From the past until now, I have sacrificed my life countless times. There were times when I was reborn as a cruel robber, as a wild bird, or as an animal where I lived solely to accumulate wealth or pursue base desires. But now, I am willing to sacrifice myself to uphold moral integrity. I do not regret my body or my life sacrificed to uphold these principles, as it brings immeasurable benefits compared to merely protecting myself and violating prohibitions. In this way of thinking, I have decided that I must sacrifice my body to protect and uphold these moral principles.

ii. Previous Life as the Son of a Butcher

This story recounts that once, a destined Bodhisattva[21] was born into a family of butchers. Upon reaching adulthood, although he desired to become a steward, he did not wish to harm animals. One day, his parents gave him a knife and a sheep, saying, "If you do not kill this sheep, we will not provide you with food and drink to sustain your life, nor will you see the sun and moon."

He thought to himself, "If I kill this sheep, I will create negative karma that will follow me for lifetimes. How can I commit such a grave sin simply for my own benefit?" He then took the knife and committed suicide. When his parents opened the door, they found the sheep standing unharmed, while their son lay lifeless.

Immediately upon death, he was reborn in a heavenly realm due to his joyous relinquishment, without regretting sacrificing his own life to uphold moral integrity.

The practice of animal release is a Buddhist method aimed at saving animals, such as fish and birds, from regular slaughter or captivity. They are released as if granted a new lease on life. This practice illustrates the fundamental Buddhist doctrine of compassion towards all sentient beings.

iii. Janasandha's Previous Life

This story, recounted by the Buddha to King Kosala, is about Prince Janasandha, the son of King Brahmadatta of Benares:

When Prince Janasandha reached adulthood and completed his education in Takkasila, he returned home. The king granted amnesty to all prisoners and appointed the prince as the deputy ruler. After the king passed away, Prince Janasandha ascended the throne and immediately ordered the construction of six alms camps for the poor. There, day after day, the king distributed six hundred coins and encouraged the entire population to practice generosity. The prison gates were permanently opened, and there were no more places of punishment for criminals.

iv. The Previous Life of Muga Pakkha

This story,[23] told by the Buddha to his disciples, explains clearly how punishment can affect both the executioner and the one directly punished. The story is about a unique prince of the king of Kasi named Temiya-kumaro (shortened to Temiya).

When Prince Temiya came of age, he was dressed beautifully

and presented before the king. Seeing his beloved son, the king embraced him and played with him. At that moment, four thieves were brought before the king; one of them was sentenced by the prince to be whipped a thousand times with a sharp-spiked whip, another was put in iron chains, another was pierced with a spear, and the last one was impaled through the body with a stake.

The Bodhisattva (Prince Temiya) heard his royal father say this and secretly thought with horror, "Oh, my father, for being a king, is accumulating such evil karma that will cause suffering in hell."

Fully aware of the consequences his father would face and fearing the same fate if he were to succeed to the throne and act similarly, Temiya resolved to pretend to be dumb and deaf for sixteen years (because he did not want to inherit the throne).

Finally, Temiya achieved his wish when he became an ascetic monk, leaving the royal palace, and then returned to teach and convert his entire royal family and many others to follow him.

This story parallels the life story of Lord Buddha, who grew up in the royal palace but then renounced the world.

3. Majjhima Nikàya Sūtra

The Angulimala Sūtra (Majjhima Sūtra number 152)[24] is a famous scripture illustrating the power of repentance and transformation.

There was a notorious bandit and murderer named Angulimala (which means "finger necklace," as he made a necklace out of the fingers of his victims). Naturally, the villagers were terrified of Angulimala. At that time, the Buddha was staying in this village and decided to go alone down the road where the notorious murderer Angulimala was said to be hiding. With his exceptional compassion, the Buddha skillfully pacified Angulimala and accepted him as a disciple.

Meanwhile, because of public outcry, the King had ordered his soldiers to capture Angulimala. The King coincidentally met the Buddha and explained the situation. Right then, the Buddha showed the King that Angulimala had transformed and was living a peaceful life as a monk. The King was completely astonished to witness this. He was amazed at how the Buddha could have transformed Angulimala in such a way.

This illustrates the concept of repentance in Buddhism. Repentance and capital punishment are mutually exclusive concepts. Nevertheless, in terms of karmic consequences, Angulimala still carried the heavy karma of his past murders, so he certainly had to endure a painful, sudden death due to this karma. However, the essence of repentance is the main theme of this scripture.

Repentance has the power to help criminals recognize their wrongdoings and strive to avoid repeating them in the future. According to Buddhism, a repentant criminal, even a murderer, can still awaken to their Buddha nature. For society, reforming criminals means reclaiming a potentially useful member who can contribute to the public welfare in some way.

B. Mahayana Scriptures

i. Avatamsaka, Sūtra (also known as the Mahāvaipulya Buddhāvataṃsaka Sūtra)

The exploration of capital punishment in the Avatamsaka, Sūtra is emblematic and philosophically profound.

The Sūtra tells of a Bodhisattva named Sudhana Sresthidaraka, who traveled seeking spiritual teachings. One of his spiritual mentors was King Anala.

King Anala lived in a splendid and distant castle. To maintain social order, the King often used magical illusions to manifest intense and painful punishments upon criminals, to deter the populace from committing crimes.

In reality, the King never harmed anyone, as both the prisoners and their punishments were merely illusory transformations created by divine powers. The King explained to Sudhana Sresthidaraka that these magical displays were a compassionate means to instill fear in people's minds, thereby dissuading them from committing sins or daring to transgress the law.

ii. The Brahmajālasuttaṃ

In the **Brahmajālasuttaṃ**,[25] the Buddha said, "Whenever a Bodhisattva sees someone preparing to harm a living being, they should skillfully use compassionate means to redeem and liberate it from suffering and misery..."

Additionally, in the twentieth chapter among the ranks of Bodhisattvas, the Buddha further taught, "If you are a disciple of the Buddha, you should engage in acts of liberating life out of compassion. Consider all males as your fathers and all females as your mothers. Throughout many lifetimes, we have all been born among them. Therefore, all sentient beings in the six realms are our fathers and mothers. If we kill them for food, we are killing our fathers and mothers, and also killing our former selves. All beings in the fourfold assembly are our true selves and bodies, therefore we should frequently engage in acts of liberating life and encourage others to do so. If you see someone intending to harm living beings, seek ways to rescue them from suffering."

C.The Great Vehicle Treatise

Rajaparikatha-ratnamala [26]:

Nagarjuna (2nd or 3rd century CE) was a renowned Buddhist philosopher from South India and also the author of the treatise Rajaparikatha-ratnamala (Precious Advice for Kings). This treatise discusses the art of leadership in the spirit of Buddhism. Long Tho advises King Udayi (of the Satavahana dynasty) on various issues [28]. Among them, Long Tho addresses capital punishment as follows:

"O Great King, due to your compassionate heart, You should always foster the intention to help all sentient beings, Even those who have committed serious offenses. Pay great attention, furthermore, To those who commit murder and create great evil; Forget not that your compassionate heart is boundless. After assessing the cruel deeds of murderers and understanding their root causes, Punishment should only be banishment, not execution or severe punishment." [29]

XI. Buddhist Kings of India

i. Buddhist King (Northern India)

a) King Aśoka [30], one of the earliest rulers of ancient India, rejected the use of military force and instead promoted the philosophy of nonviolence and respect for all people.

King Aśoka's edicts, inscribed on pillars, reveal him as a visionary ruler ahead of his time. Below is a summary of some of King Aśoka's edicts:

Prohibitions:

- No use of animals for religious sacrifices.
- Prohibition of all animal and livestock slaughter.
- The king will no longer organize hunting expeditions.
- The king renounces the glory of conquest.
- Victory through righteousness is the most glorious achievement.

Public Works:

- Construction of hospitals for people and animals.
- Establishment of many herbal gardens.
- Digging of wells, planting of trees, and building of rest houses along roads to provide convenience for pilgrims and animals.

Human Relationships:

- People must obey their parents and spiritual teachers.
- Employers should not mistreat their servants and employees.
- Everyone should be generous to monks, relatives, and friends.

Religion:

- Religious sects "may reside everywhere."
- Followers of different beliefs should not attack each other when "studying other religions."

Welfare for the People:

- Government officials must care for the elderly, the poor, and prisoners.
- Officials reporting on public works can have direct audience with the king at any time and place.
- Officials must ensure that the administration effectively benefits and brings happiness to the people.

Justice:

- Judges must be independent and consistent in their procedures and sentencing.
- Offenders should be given as much leniency as possible.
- The death penalty should be limited and convictions should have a three-day period before sentencing.
- "Not killing is a virtuous act."

In the final edict, possibly written in 242 BCE, King Aśoka wrote: "In the world, there are two ways to achieve righteousness: law and faith."

However, among these two, it seems that law proves to be less effective than faith. "Specially trained officials, called dhamma-mahamattas (Great Officers for the Promotion of Dharma), frequently travel to understand the perspectives of the people and guide them in righteousness.

This makes it clear that King Aśoka supported the spirit of nonviolence (ahimsa) and was opposed to the application of the death penalty. He was a devout Buddhist dedicated to righteous conduct and thus could not permit executions to take place.

b) In the sixth century, two Chinese pilgrim monks, Sung Yun and Hui Sheng, visited India and wrote as follows:

We entered the country of Ouchang (Oudyana). The northern part of this country borders the Thong Ling mountains; the southern part borders India... The king of this country was very devout and practiced vegetarianism... After lunch, the king personally attended to state affairs.

If someone committed murder, they were not executed but exiled to deserted islands, provided with just enough food to sustain their lives. After an assessment, the punishment was adjusted according to the severity and circumstances of each case[31].

ii. Buddhist King (Central India)

Fa Xian (337-422), an early Chinese pilgrim monk who visited India, mentioned the Buddhist king of Central India as follows:

The king of Central India ruled without the use of capital punishment (i.e., the death penalty) or corporal punishment. Criminals were simply fined, with the severity of the fine depending on the circumstances of each case. Even in cases of severe rebellion, the punishment was limited to cutting off the right hand. Throughout the country, people refrained from killing, drunkenness, and consuming pungent and strong-smelling foods like onions and garlic[32].

iii. Buddhist King (Central Region of India)

In the eighth century, the Korean monk Hye Ch'o, who visited India about three centuries after Fa Xian, described the Buddhist kings of the central region of India as ruling without the use of the death penalty:

"The national laws in the five regions of India stipulate that there is no chaining, beating, or imprisonment depending on the severity of the crime. There is no death penalty"[33].

iv. Buddhist King (Western India)

Venerable Hye Ch'o noted a similar situation in Western India:

"There are no chains, beatings, imprisonment, executions, or similar punishments here"[34].

Japanese Emperor

In 724 CE, Japanese Emperor Shomu (724-749), a devout Buddhist following the Kegon sect, built the famous Todai-ji temple in the city of Nara and abolished the death penalty. This occurred at the end of the Nara period (715-794). Similarly, throughout the Heian period (794-1185), the death penalty was rarely enforced[35].

The Dalai Lama of Tibet

The 13th Dalai Lama of Tibet, Thubten Gyatso (1876-1933), the predecessor of the current 14th Dalai Lama, Tenzin Gyatso (born 1935), fought to modernize Tibet and maintain national sovereignty against British and later Chinese influence. He also reformed the feudal legal system of Tibet. One of these reforms was the abolition of the death penalty around 1920. Before that, the Dalai Lama often refrained from directly intervening in cases of capital punishment due to his religious role.[36]

XII. Practical Application

It is evident that every person possesses inherent potential; thus, the focus should be on training and unlocking this potential. We should not succumb to unwholesome emotions or violence. Solutions aimed at transforming individuals' thinking are more practical than creating confrontation and conflict.

The death penalty is not the best solution to prevent people from committing crimes. It is merely a temporary deterrent. Implementing such a harsh measure is neither meaningful nor appropriate, as it undermines the principles of compassion and kindness.

A meaningful and appropriate action would be: when a person commits a crime, they should be either imprisoned or placed under house arrest for a certain period, allowing them time to reform. The individual may recognize their wrongdoing and develop remorse. Since humans are conscious beings, even wrongdoers can feel shame for their actions. To help them improve their behavior, we must prioritize education and promote human values through religious ethics or healthy social programs.

We need to support education more and encourage a collective sense of responsibility. We should also explain the importance of practicing compassion and kindness for personal benefit and strive to minimize factors that nurture violent tendencies, such as the proliferation of weapons in our societies.

To facilitate the individual's transformation, we should propose several specific methods:

1. The individual should live in isolation for a period, such as one or two months, or even one or two years, to reflect on and repent for their actions.
2. Encourage the individual to engage in good deeds that benefit others.
3. The individual should practice daily meditation to transform unwholesome actions into wholesome ones.
4. The individual must self-examine the roots of their wrongful actions.
5. Wrongful actions can stem from murder, robbery, adultery, deceit, or the use of alcohol and drugs.
6. The method to address wrongful actions is to practice the Noble Eightfold Path: right view, right intention, right

speech, right action, right livelihood, right effort, right mindfulness, and right concentration.

7. The individual can potentially become a good person as they were before.

Buddhism is a path for transforming suffering. We can all be influenced by negative emotions and unwholesome thoughts, whether guilty or not. However, by applying the aforementioned educational methods in daily life, we can reap the benefits of peace and happiness here and now in our current life. Prevention is better than intervention, and education should occur before punishment is necessary. A good cause often produces a good result.

This is a truth pervasive throughout Buddhist scriptures. Buddhism takes a strong stance against killing in general, and in certain cases, against the death penalty.

Thus, the Buddha completely rejected the death penalty. No true Buddhist supports capital punishment. However, we should understand that the teachings in Buddhism are not dogmatic but are the fruits of wisdom. These are simple pieces of advice from the Buddha, with clear explanations of why we should not kill, primarily based on moral grounds and related to the law of karma.

The Buddhist stance against the death penalty is grounded in Buddhist philosophy and aligns with societal realities.

Firstly, there is a possibility that the death penalty in national legal systems could lead to wrongful executions of innocent people, a common occurrence even in advanced countries like the United States. Once carried out, the death penalty is irreversible and cannot be rectified if the accused is later proven innocent.

Secondly, Buddhism believes that fundamentally, everyone is inherently good, and the primary aim of Buddhism is education, transformation, and reform, not destruction. If someone is ill, Buddhism strives to cure the illness rather than eliminate the patient. Buddhism views criminals as individuals with mental issues combined with ignorance (avidya).

Thus, the primary aim of Buddhism is to eradicate the root of ignorance rather than destroy the ignorant. This can be achieved through a system of education, transformation, and reform of the individual, in other words, helping the individual see things as they truly are.

In Buddhism, there is a saying: "Even building nine pagodas is not as valuable as saving one person's life."

In summary, based on the fundamental teachings of the Buddha from Buddhist scriptures and the compassionate and enlightened mindset of the Buddhist kings in ancient Asian history as mentioned above, we wholeheartedly support the call to world leaders who still apply the death penalty to abolish this punishment in the boundless compassion of Buddhism.

***

[1] http://quangduc.com/English/canon/vinaya/05.bikkhu-rules-guide.html#5precepts; http://www.unfetteredmind.org/articles/precept1.php;

[2] The Brahma Net Sūtra, trans. by the Buddhist Text Translation Society in USA, xem http://www.purifymind.com/BrahmaNetSūtra.htm

[3] Dhammasaṇganī Aṭṭhakathā (Atthasālinī), ed. E. Müller, 1897, PTS, p. 129; Saddhammo pāyana, ed. Richard Morris, V, PTS, 1887, p. 58; Kaṇkhāvitaranī, ed. D. A. L. Maskell (néc stede), 1957, PTS, p. 50.

[4] Dhammasaṇganī Aṭṭhakathā (Atthasālinī), ed. E. Müller, 1897, PTS, p. 129; Kaṇkhāvitaranī, ed. D. A. L. Maskell (néc stcdc), 1957, PTS, p. 30.

[5] The Brahma Net Sūtra, trans. by the Buddhist Text

Translation Society in USA, xem http://www.purifymind.com/BrahmaNetSūtra.htm

[6] Khuddhaka Nikaya (belong to the Sutta Nipata), tr. By Thanissaro Bhikkhu, I.8, Karanaiya Metta Sutta.

[7] The Lotus Sūtra, tr. By Burton Watson, Colombia Univeristy Press, New York, 1993, pp 10-11.

[8] Brahma Net Sūtra, I, 162.

[9] Bồ tát nguyện giữ giới "Không sát hại người và súc vật".

[10] Cherishing Life, I, 83.

[11] Cherishing Life, II, 5.

[12] Dhammapada, tran. by Thanissaro Bhikkhu, Verse 5 of Chapter 1, MA 01005, USA, 1997.

[13] http://www.vipassana.com/canon/majjhima/mn135.php

[14] Mullin, Glenn H., Death and Dying: The Tibtant Tradition, Boston: Arkana Penguin, 1986, p. 17.

[15] Telakaṭāhagāthā, v, 78.

[16] http://www.vipassana.com/canon/majjhima/mn135.php

[17] Dhammapada, tran. by Thanissaro Bhikkhu, verses no 129 of Chapter 10, MA 01005, USA, 1997.

[18] Nt, verses no 130 of Chapter 10.

[19] Nt, verses no 405 of Chapter 26.

[20] Jataka, ed. V. Fausboll, London: PTS, 1962; ed. E.B. Cowell, tr. By Robert Chalmers, Stories of the Buddha's Former Births, I, Story Banian, Low Price Publications, Delhi-52, p. 149.

[21] Thánh Dự lưu còn gọi Nhập Lưu hoặc bảy lần tái sanh ở đời nữa.

[22] The Jataka or Stories of the Buddha's Former Births,

Vol. 4, Bk. 12 (E.B. Cowell, ed.; W.H.D. Rouse, trans. 1957) pp. 109-11.

[23] The Jataka or Stories of the Buddha's Former Births, Vol. 6, Bk. 22, pp.1-19.

[24] The Collection of the Middle Length Sayings (Majjhima-Nikaya), Isaline B. Horner, trans. 1957, pp. 284-92. See also, Hellmuth Hecker, Angulimala: A Murder's Road to Sainthood (The Wheel Publication No. 312, 1984).

[25] Brahma Net Sūtra, I, 162. See http://www.ymba.org/bns/bnsframe.htm.

[26] Nagarjuna and Kaysang Gyatso [Dalai Lama VII], The Precious Garland and The Song of the Four Mindfulnesses (Jeffrey Hopkins et al, trans., 1975).

[27] The Encyclopedia of Eastern Philosophy and Religion, pp. 237-38.

[28] For an interpretation of the text and some background on King Udayi, see Robert A.F. Thurman, "Nagarjuna's Guidelines for Buddhist Social Action," in The Path of Compassion: Writings on Socially Engaged Buddhism (Fred Eppsteiner, ed. 1988); Robert A.F. Thurman, "Social and Cultural Rights in Buddhism," in Human Rights and the World's Religions (Leroy S. Rouner, ed. 1988), p. 148. A brief overview of the Satavahana Dynasty can be found in Rama Shankar Tripathi, History of Ancient India (1942), pp.191-201; Etienne Lamotte, History of Indian Buddhism: From the Origins to the Saka Era (Sara Webb Boin and Jean Dantinne, trans. 1988), pp. 474-81.

[29] The Precious Garland and the Song of the Four Mindfulnessess, pp. 66-67.

[30] Aśoka Rock and Pillar Edicts, the translation by Ven. S. Dhammika, Kandy, Sri Lanka; Buddhist Publication Society, 1993. See http://www.thenagain.info/Classes/Sources/Aśoka.html

[31] Travels of Fah-Hian and Sung Yun, Buddhist Pilgrims

from China to India (400 A.D. and 518 A.D.), pp. 188-89.

[32] A Record of Buddhist Kingdoms: Being an Account by the Chinese Monk Fa-Hieh of His Travels in India and Ceylon, p. 43.

[33] Hye Ch'o, The Hye Ch'o Diary: Memoir of the Pilgrimage to the Five Regions of India (Yang Han-Sung et al, trans. and ed. 1980) pp. 40-41. Also see, Damien P. Horigan, A Buddhist Perspective on the Death Penalty of Compassion and Capital Punishment, The American Journal of Jurisprudence, Volume 41(1996), p. 271-288

[34] Như trên

[35] Damien P. Horigan, A Buddhist Perspective on the Death Penalty of Compassion and Capital Punishment, The American Journal of Jurisprudence, Volume 41 (1996), p. 286.

[36] Franz Michael, Rule by Incarnation: Tibetan Buddhism and Its Role in Society and State (1982), pp. 70, 109. For a glimpse of the traditional Tibetan criminal justice system, see Rebecca Redwood French, The Golden Yoke: The Legal Cosmology of Buddhist Tibet (1995), pp. 315-25.

REFERENCE SOURCE

- Anguttara Nikāya (Tăng Chi Bộ). Translated by the Most Ven. Thích Minh Châu.
- Dìgha Nikàya (Trường Bộ kinh). English Trans. By Pali Text Society.
- Saṃyutta Nikāya (Tương Ưng Bộ Kinh) II. Translated by the Most Ven. Thích Minh Châu. Published by Buddhist Studies in Vietnam Research Institute. 1993.
- Khuddaka Nikāya (Tiểu Bộ), Sutta 536, The Story of the Bird Lord Kunāla (Chuyện Chúa Chim Kunāla). Translated by the Most Ven. Thích Minh Châu.
- Dìghàgama (Kinh Trường A-hàm). Sutra Wandering (Kinh Du hành). Chinese trans. by Buddhayaśsa. Vietnamese trans. by the Most Ven. Tue Sy.
- Suttanipata (Kinh Tập) Chapter 3: Samyutta Kosala. II: Chapter Two 3.14–15. Two Words About War (Hai Lời Nói Về Chiến Tranh
- The Great Treasure Sūtra (Kinh Đại Bảo Tích)
- https://phatphapungdung.com/phap-bao/kinh-dai-bao-tich-123383.html
- Brahmajāla Sutta: The All-embracing Net of Views (Kinh Phạm Võng). Translated from the Pali by Bhikkhu Bodhi. 2010. Alternate translation: Thanissaro
- https://www.accesstoinsight.org/tipitaka/dn/dn.01.0.bodh.html
- The Śūraṅgama Sūtra. Chinese trans. by Pramiti. Vietnamese trans. by Tam Minh Le Dinh Tham. Published

by Phật Học Viện Quốc Tế. 1983.

    - https://ngaynay.vn/phatgiao/loi-phat-day-ve-qua-bao-dang-so-cua-nghiep-giet-hai-chung-sanh-post123743.html
    - https://www.huongsentemple.com/LuanHoiTrongLangKinhLangNghiem.pdf

- The Buddha's Teaching of the Mahayana Infinite Life Dignified Pure Equality Enlightenment Sūtra (Phật Thuyết Đại Thừa Vô Lượng Thọ Trang Nghiêm Thanh Tịnh Bình Đẳng Giác Kinh).Chinese translated by Hạ Liên Cư (hội tập). Vietnamese trans. by Thích Đức Niệm & Minh Chánh. Tôn Giáo Publishing. Hà Nội. 2009.
    - https://ph.tinhtong.vn/Home/Doc/phuc-giang-kinh-vo-luong-tho-lan-2-co-luu-to-van-000037?t=4
- Mahàprajnàparamitàsatra (Luận Đại Trí Độ). Nàgàrjuna (Long Thọ). Trans from Sanskrit to Chinese: Kumārajīva. Trans from Chinese into Vietnamese: Thích Thiện Siêu. Published by Buddhist Studies in Vietnam Research Institute. 1997.
- Dhammapada. Trans by Thích Minh Châu
    - https://phatphapungdung.com/kinh-phap-cu-pham-song-yeu-cau-4-201977.html
- Thích Nhất Hạnh (2003). Creating True Peace: Ending Violence in Yourself, Your Family, Your Community, and the World. Free Press.
- Paul R. Fleischman (2002). The Buddha Taught Nonviolence, Not Pacifism. Pariyatti Publishing.
- Mahatma Gandhi (1942). Nonviolence in peace & war (1942-49. Navajivan Publishing House.
- Thích Nhất Hạnh (1993). Love In Action: Writings on Nonviolent Social Change. Parallax Press
- Keown, Damien (1992). The Nature of Buddhist Ethics.

London: Macmillan.

- Keown, Damien (1992). Bản Chất Đạo Đức Phật Giáo. Luân Đôn: Macmillan.
- Ñānamoli, Bhikkhu (1992). The Life of the Buddha. Seattle: BPS Pariyatti.
- Ñānamoli, Tỳ khưu (1992). Cuộc Đời Đức Phật. Seattle: BPS Pariyatti.
- Nyantiloka (1972). A Buddhist Dictionary: Manual of Buddhist Terms and Doctrines. Colombo: Frewin & Co., Ltd.
- Nyantiloka (1972). Từ điển Phật giáo: Cẩm nang về Thuật ngữ và Giáo lý Phật giáo. Colombo: Frewin & Co., Ltd.
- Ten Paramitas. Temiya Jàtaka. The Story of Temiya Boddhisatta practices the Paramitas of Renunciation. Bhikkhu Hộ Tông (Vansarakkhita Maha Thera)
    - https://www.budsas.org/uni/u-thapdo/thapdo-03.htm
- Metta Sutta. Discourse On Loving-kindness.
    - https://www.huongsentemple.com/index.php/vn/phat-phap/kinh-ta-ng-ca-a-cha-a-hs/6256-nghi-le-hang-ngay-20
- Thích Thắng Hoan. Đức Phật- Nhà đại Cách Mạng,
    - https://thuvienhoasen.org/a33850/duc-phat-nha-dai-cach-mang
- Nandasena Ratnapala. Sự Phân Tầng Xã Hội. TKN. Hằng Liên dịch
    - https://daophatkhatsi.vn/phat-giao-cac-nganh/phat-giao-va-xa-hoi-hoc/su-phan-tang-xa-hoi.html
- Ravi Shankar Sing. Ảnh hưởng của Phong Trào Phục Hưng Phật giáo của B.R. Ambedkar vào việc phát triển Kinh Tế-Xã Hội của tầng lớp Tiện Dân ở Ấn Độ.

    - http://hoangphap.info/Page.aspx?ArticleID=6081&SubID=5&ID=6
- Martin Luther King: Cuộc đời và Sự nghiệp qua Ảnh.
    - https://www.luatkhoa.com/2017/01/martin-luther-king-cuoc-doi-va-su-nghiep-qua-anh/
- H.G. Wells (1866–1946), A Short History of the World. 1922.
- Viết Hiền, Spring of a Saint - a Great Soul (Mùa Xuân của một vị Thánh - một Tâm Hồn Vĩ Đại).
    - https://baobinhdinh.vn/562/2003/2/1967/
- Dr. Ram Ponnu, Ahimsa: Its theory and practice in Gandhism.
    - https://www.mkgandhi.org/articles/ahimsa-Its-theory-and-practice-in-Gandhism.html
- John Dear, The Experiments of Gandhi: Nonviolence In The Nuclear Age, Gandhi Journal, August, 2009.
    - https://www.mkgandhi.org/articles/ahimsa-Its-theory-and-practice-in-Gandhism.html
- His Holiness the Dalai Lama, An Icon of Ahimsa - Mahatma Gandhi (1869–1948). Published by India Today on August 21, 2021
    - https://www.dalailama.com/messages/transcripts-and-interviews/an-icon-ofahimsa-mahatma-gandhi-1869-1948
- Ambedkar – the Person rekindled the Light of Buddhism (Ambedkar - Người thắp sáng lại ngọn lửa Phật pháp)
- Theo phatphap.org.vn
    - https://fos.ussh.vnu.edu.vn/vi/news/tan-man-phuong-dong/ambedkar-nguoi-thap-sang-lai-ngon-lua-phat-phap-150.html
- Ravi Shankar Sing, The influence of B.R.Ambedkar's

Buddhist revival movement on the socio-economic development of the untouchables in India (Ảnh hưởng của phong trào phục hưng Phật giáo của B.R.Ambedkar vào việc phát triển kinh tế-xã hội của tầng lớp tiện dân ở Ấn Độ).

  - http://hoangphap.info/Page.aspx?ArticleID=6081&SubID=5&ID=6

- Ambedkar – the Person rekindled the Light of Buddhism (Ambedkar - Người thắp sáng lại ngọn lửa Phật pháp)
- Theo phatphap.org.vn
  - https://fos.ussh.vnu.edu.vn/vi/news/tan-man-phuong-dong/ambedkar-nguoi-thap-sang-lai-ngon-lua-phat-phap-150.html
- Unknown author. The Letter "Heartfelt prayer" of Bodhisattva Thich Quang Duc before self-immolation (Bức thư "Lời nguyện tâm huyết" của Bồ Tát Thich Quang Duc trước khi tự thiêu).
  - https://quangduc.com/a6759/buc-thu-loi-nguyen-tam-huyet-cua-bo-tat-thich-quang-duc-truoc-khi-tu-thieu
- Trần Văn Giàu, The South kept its Citadel (Miền Nam giữ vững thành đồng), Vol II. Publishing Khoa học, Hà Nội, 1966, tr. 342.
  - https://thuvienhoasen.org/a13472/suc-manh-bat-bao-dong-nhin-tu-ngon-lua-thich-quang-duc-le-cung
- "I Have A Dream" Speech by Dr. Martin Luther King, Jr. March on Washington for Jobs and Freedom. August 28, 1963.
  - https://www.marshall.edu/onemarshallu/i-have-a-dream/
- Minh Duc Trieu Tam Anh, A lowly caste girl felt in love Venerable Ānanda (Cô Gái Hạ Tiện Yêu Tôn Giả

Ānanda): One Life, One Sun and Moon (Một cuộc đời, Một vầng nhật nguyệt). Episode 6. Publishing House: Văn Học. 2014.

- https://thuvienhoasen.org/a21264/co-gai-ha-tien-yeu-ton-gia-nanda

- K. R. Norman, Buddhism and Aśoka King (Phật Giáo và A-dục Vương).
- Châu Thành, Bodhisattva Thich Quang Duc His Will to Heart (Bồ Tát Thich Quang Duc Từ Lời Nguyện Đến Trái Tim)
  - https://thuvienhoasen.org/a17333/bo-tat-thich-quang-duc-tu-loi-nguyen-den-trai-tim
- 80 Martin Luther King Jr. Quotes That Inspire Courage, Peace, and Justice (80 Câu Trích Dẫn Của Martin Luther King Jr Truyền Cảm Hứng Về Lòng Dũng Cảm, Hòa Bình Và Sự Công Bằng). Collected by Hoàng Thị Thùy Dung.
  - https://ivolunteervietnam.com/80-cau-trich-dan-cua-martin-luther-king-jr-truyen-cam-hung-ve-long-dung-cam-hoa-binh-va-su-cong-bang.html
- Thích Trí Giải, The Nature of Violence Between Religions and the Nonviolent Spirit of Buddhism (Tính Chất Bạo Động Giữa Các Tôn Giáo và Tinh Thần Bất Bạo Động Của Phật Giáo).
  - http://www.phatgiaodaichung.com/Bai2011_04/002batbaodong.htm
- Thich Duc Truong, The Message of Vesak in April (Thông điệp tháng Tư).
  - https://phatgiao.vn/bai-viet/thong-diep-thang-tu.html
- Collection of articles about King Aśoka and Vietnamese trans by Nguyên Tâm.
  - https://quangduc.com/a27861/Aśoka-cuoc-doi-va-su-

nghiep-tuyen-tap-cac-bai-viet-ve-vua-a-duc

- Dr. Ram Ponnu. Ahimsa: Its theory and practice in Gandhism.
- https://www.mkgandhi.org/articles/ahimsa-Its-theory-and-practice-in-Gandhism.html
- Ahimsa in Encyclopaedia Britannica
- https://www.britannica.com/topic/ahimsa
- Ahimsa in Wikipedia
- https://en.wikipedia.org/wiki/Ahimsa
- https://vi.wikipedia.org
- MartinLutherKingJr.com
- Photos and information from Giác Ngộ Online, Google, and other websites

BAO ANH LAC BOOKSHELF

Dr. Bhikṣuṇī TN Giới Hương composed

1.1. THE VIETNAMESE BOOKS

1. *Bồ-tát và Tánh Không Trong Kinh Tạng Pali và* Đại *Thừa* (Boddhisattva and Sunyata in the Early and Developed Buddhist Traditions).
2. *Ban Mai Xứ Ấn* (The Dawn in India) - *Tuyển tập các Tiểu Luận Phật Giáo* (Collection of Buddhist Essays), (3 tập).
3. *Vườn Nai – Chiếc Nôi* (Phật Giáo Deer Park–The Cradle of Buddhism).
4. *Quy Y Tam Bảo và Năm Giới* (Take Refuge in Three Gems and Keep the Five Precepts).
5. *Vòng Luân Hồi* (The Cycle of Life).
6. *Hoa Tuyết Milwaukee* (Snowflake in Milwaukee).
7. *Luân Hồi trong Lăng Kính Lăng Nghiêm* (The Rebirth in Śūrangama Sūtra).
8. *Nghi Thức Hộ Niệm, Cầu Siêu* (The Ritual for the Deceased).
9. *Quan* Âm *Quảng Trần* (The Commentary of Avalokiteśvara Bodhisattva).
10. *Nữ Tu và Tù Nhân Hoa Kỳ* (A Nun and American Inmates).
11. *Nếp Sống Tỉnh Thức của Đức Đạt Lai Lạt Ma Thứ XIV* (The Awakened Mind of the 14th Dalai Lama).
12. *A-Hàm: Mưa pháp chuyển hóa phiền não* (*Agama – A Dharma Rain transforms the Defilement*), 2 tập.
13. *Góp Từng Hạt Nắng Perris* (Collection of Sunlight in Perris).

14. *Pháp Ngữ của Kinh Kim Cang* (The Key Words of Vajracchedikā-Prajñāpāramitā-Sūtra).
15. *Tập Thơ Nhạc Nắng Lăng Nghiêm* (Songs and Poems of Śūraṅgama Sunlight).
16. *Nét Bút Bên Song Cửa* (Reflections at the Temple Window).
17. *Máy Nghe MP3 Hương Sen* (Hương Sen Digital Mp3 Radio Speaker): Các Bài Giảng, Sách, Bài viết và Thơ Nhạc của Thích Nữ Giới Hương (383/201 bài).
18. *DVD Giới Thiệu về Chùa* Hương Sen, USA (Introduction on Huong Sen Temple).
19. *Ni Giới Việt Nam Hoằng Pháp tại Hoa Kỳ* (Sharing the Dharma - Vietnamese Buddhist Nuns in the United States).
20. *Tuyển Tập 40 Năm Tu Học & Hoằng Pháp của Ni sư Giới* Hương (Forty Years in the Dharma: A Life of Study and Service—Venerable Bhikkhuni Giới Hương), Thích Nữ Viên Quang, TN Viên Nhuận, TN Viên Tiến, and TN Viên Khuông.
21. *Tập Thơ Nhạc Lối Về Sen Nở (Songs and Poems of Lotus Blooming on the Way).*
22. *Nghi Thức* Công Phu *Khuya – Thần Chú Thủ Lăng Nghiêm* (Śūraṅgama Mantra).
23. *Nghi Thức Cầu An – Kinh Phổ* Môn (The Universal Door Sūtra).
24. *Nghi Thức Cầu An – Kinh Dược Sư* (The Medicine Buddha Sūtra).
25. *Nghi Thức Sám Hối Hồng Danh* (The Sūtra of Confession at many Buddha Titles).
26. *Nghi Thức* Công Phu *Chiều – Mông* Sơn *Thí Thực* (The Ritual Donating Food to Hungry Ghosts).
27. *Khóa Tịnh* Độ *– Kinh A Di* Đà (The Amitabha Buddha Sūtra).
28. *Nghi Thức Cúng Linh và Cầu Siêu* (The Rite for Deceased and Funeral Home).

29. *Nghi Lễ Hàng Ngày - 50 Kinh Tụng và các Lễ* Vía *trong Năm* (The Daily Chanting Rituals and Annual Ceremonies).
30. *Hương* Đạo *Trong* Đời *2022* (Tuyển tập 60 Bài Thi trong Cuộc Thi Viết Văn Ứng Dụng Phật Pháp 2022 - A Collection of Writings on the Practicing of Buddhism in Daily Life in the Writing Contest 2022).
31. *Hương Pháp 2022* (Tuyển Tập Các Bài Thi Trúng Giải Cuộc Thi Viết Văn Ứng Dụng Phật Pháp 2022 - A Collection of the Winning Writings on the Practicing of Buddhism in Daily Life in the Writing Contest 2022).
32. *Giới* Hương - *Thơm Ngược Gió Ngàn* (Giới Hương – The Virtue Fragrance Against the Thousand Winds), Nguyên Hà.
33. *Pháp Ngữ Kinh Hoa Nghiêm* (Buddha-avatamsaka-nāma-mahāvaipulya-sūtra) (2 tập).
34. *Tinh Hoa Kinh Hoa Nghiêm (The Core of Buddha-avatamsaka-nāma-mahāvaipulya-sūtra*).
35. *Phật Giáo – Tầm Nhìn Lịch Sử Và Thực Hành* (*Buddhism: A Historical and Practical Vision*). Hiệu đính: Thích Hạnh Chánh và Thích Nữ Giới Hương.
36. *Nhật ký Hành Thiền Vipassana và Kinh Tứ Niệm Xứ* (Diary: Practicing Vipassana and the Four Foundations of Mindfulness Sutta)
37. *Nghi cúng Giao Thừa* (New Year's Eve Ceremony)
38. *Nghi cúng Rằm Tháng Giêng* (the Ceremony of the First Month's Full Moon)
39. *Nghi thức Lễ Phật* Đản (The Buddha Birthday's Ceremony)
40. *Nghi thức Vu Lan* (The Ullambana Festival or Parent Day)
41. *Lễ* Vía Quan Âm *(*The Avolokiteshvara Day)
42. *Nghi cúng Thánh Tổ Kiều* Đàm *Di* (The Death Anniversary of Mahapajapati Gotami)
43. *Nghi thức cúng Tổ và Giác linh Sư trưởng* (The Ancestor Day)

44. *Nghi Lễ Chẩn Tế Mười Hai Loại Cô Hồn* (Offering Food to the Twelve Ghosts)
45. *Kỷ Yếu Lễ Tưởng Niệm Thánh Tổ Kiều* Đàm *Di tại Chùa* Hương Sen *năm 2024* (The Yearbook of the Commemoration of Mahapajapati Gotami at Huong Sen Temple in 2024)
46. *Nghi Thức Cầu Siêu Chư* Hương Linh Thai Nhi (Pray for the Abortion, Unborn Baby)
47. *Kim Quang Minh Kinh Sám Trai Thiên Khóa Nghi (The Golden Light Sutra - Heavenly Course)*
48. *Phật Giáo và Thánh Tích Sri Lanka* (Buddhism and Holy Buddhist Places in Sri Lanka)

1.2. THE ENGLISH BOOKS

1. *Boddhisattva and Sunyata in the Early and Developed Buddhist Traditions.*
2. *Rebirth Views in the* Śūraṅgama *Sūtra.*
3. *Commentary of Avalokiteśvara Bodhisattva.*
4. *The Key Words in Vajracchedikā Sūtra.*
5. *Sārnātha-The Cradle of Buddhism in the Archeological View.*
6. *Take Refuge in the Three Gems and Keep the Five Precepts.*
7. *Cycle of Life.*
8. *Forty Years in the Dharma: A Life of Study and Service—Venerable Bhikkhuni Giới* Hương.
9. *Sharing the Dharma -Vietnamese Buddhist Nuns in the United States.*
10. *A Vietnamese Buddhist Nun and American Inmates.*
11. *Daily Monastic Chanting.*
12. *Weekly Buddhist Discourse Chanting.*
13. *Practice Meditation and Pure Land.*

14. *The Ceremony for Peace.*
15. *The Lunch Offering Ritual.*
16. *The Ritual Offering Food to Hungry Ghosts.*
17. *The Pureland Course of Amitabha Sutra.*
18. *The Medicine Buddha Sutra.*
19. *The New Year Ceremony.*
20. *The Great Parinirvana Ceremony.*
21. *The Buddha's Birthday Ceremony.*
22. *The Ullambana Festival (Parents' Day).*
23. *The Marriage Ceremony.*
24. *The Blessing Ceremony for The Deceased.*
25. *The Ceremony Praising Ancestral Masters.*
26. *The Enlightened Buddha Ceremony.*
27. *The Uposatha Ceremony (Reciting Precepts).*
28. *Buddhism: A Historical and Practical Vision.* Edited by Ven. Dr. Thich Hanh Chanh and Ven. Dr. Bhikṣuṇī TN Gioi Huong.
29. *Contribution of Buddhism For World Peace & Social Harmony*. Edited by Ven. Dr. Buddha Priya Mahathero and Ven. Dr. Bhikṣuṇī TN Gioi Huong.
30. *Global Spread of Buddhism with Special Reference to Sri Lanka.* Buddhist Studies Seminar in Kandy University. Edited by Dr. Ven. Kahawatte Sumedha Thero and Dr. Bhikṣuṇī TN Gioi Huong.
31. *Buddhism In Sri Lanka During The Period of 19th to 21st Centuries*. Buddhist Studies Seminar in Colombo. Edited by Prof. Ven. Medagama Nandawansa and Dr. Bhikṣuṇī TN Gioi Huong.
32. *Diary: Practicing Vipassana and the Four Foundations of Mindfulness Sutta.*

1.3.THE BILINGUAL BOOKS (VIETNAMESE-ENGLISH)

1. *Bản Tin Hương Sen: Xuân, Phật* Đản, *Vu Lan (*Hương Sen Newsletter: Spring, Buddha Birthday and Vu Lan, annual/ Mỗi Năm).
2. *Danh Ngôn Nuôi Dưỡng Nhân Cách - Good Sentences Nurture a Good Manner.*
3. *Văn Hóa* Đặc *Sắc của Nước Nhật Bản-Exploring the Unique Culture of Japan.*
4. *Sống An Lạc dù* Đời *không* Đẹp *như Mơ - Live Peacefully though Life is not Beautiful as a Dream.*
5. *Hãy* Nói *Lời Yêu Thương-Words of Love and Understanding.*
6. *Văn Hóa Cổ Kim qua Hành* Hương *Chiêm* Bái -The Ancient-Present Culture in Pilgrim.
7. *Nghệ Thuật Biết Sống - Art of Living.*
8. *Dharamshala - Hành* Hương *Vùng* Đất *Thiêng, Ấn* Độ, *Dharamshala - Pilgrimage to the Sacred Land, India.*

1.4.THE TRANSLATED BOOKS

1. *Xá Lợi Của Đức Phật* (Relics of the Buddha), Tham Weng Yew.
2. *Sen Nở Nơi Chốn Tử Tù* (Lotus in Prison), many authors.
3. *Chùa Việt Nam Hải Ngoại* (Overseas Vietnamese Buddhist Temples).
4. *Việt Nam Danh Lam Cổ Tự* (The Famous Ancient Buddhist Temples in Vietnam).
5. *Hương Sen, Thơ và Nhạc* – (Lotus Fragrance, Poem and Music).
6. *Phật Giáo-Một Bậc* Đạo *Sư, Nhiều Truyền Thống* (Buddhism: One Teacher – Many Traditions), Đức Đạt Lai Lạt Ma 14th & Ni Sư Thubten Chodren.

7. *Cách Chuẩn Bị Chết và Giúp Người Sắp Chết-Quan* Điểm *Phật Giáo* (Preparing for Death and Helping the Dying – A Buddhist Perspective).

2. BUDDHIST MUSIC ALBUMS from POEMS of THÍCH NỮ GIỚI HƯƠNG

1. *Đào Xuân Lộng Ý Kinh* (The Buddha's Teachings Reflected in Cherry Flowers).
2. *Niềm Tin Tam Bảo* (Trust in the Three Gems).
3. *Trăng Tròn Nghìn Năm* Đón *Chờ Ai* (Who Is the Full Moon Waiting for for Over a Thousand Years?).
4. *Ánh Trăng Phật Pháp* (Moonlight of Dharma-Buddha).
5. *Bình Minh Tỉnh Thức* (Awakened Mind at the Dawn) (*Piano Variations for Meditation*).
6. *Tiếng Hát Già Lam* (Song from Temple).
7. *Cảnh Đẹp Chùa Xưa* (The Magnificent, Ancient Buddhist Temple).
8. Karaoke *Hoa* Ưu Đàm Đã *Nở* (An Udumbara Flower Is Blooming).
9. *Hương Sen Ca* (Hương Sen's Songs)
10. *Về Chùa Vui Tu* (Happily Go to Temple for Spiritual Practices)
11. *Gọi Nắng Xuân Về* (Call the Spring Sunlight).
12. Đệ *Tử Phật*. Thơ: Thích Nữ Giới Hương, Nhạc: Uy Thi Ca & Giác An, volume 4, năm 2023.

Mời xem: http://www.huongsentemple.com/index.php/kinh-sach/tu-sach-bao-anh-lac

NONVIOLENT STRUGGLE
The Foundation for Building Global Peace
Tác giả: Ven. Dr. Bhikṣuṇī Gioi Huong

NHÀ XUẤT BẢN TÔN GIÁO
53 Tràng Thi – Hoàn Kiếm - Hà Nội
ĐT: (024)37822845
Email: nhaxuatbantongiao@gmail.com

Chịu trách nhiệm xuất bản:
Giám đốc: ThS. Nguyễn Hữu Có

Chịu trách nhiệm nội dung:
Tổng Biên tập: Lê Hồng Sơn
Biên tập: Nguyễn Thị Thanh Thủy
Trình bày: Vũ Đình Trọng

Số lượng in: 1.000 bản, Khổ: 14 x 20 cm
In tại: Công ty TNHH Sản xuất Thương mại Dịch vụ In ấn Trâm Anh,
159/57 Bạch Đằng, phường 2, quận Tân Bình, thành phố Hồ Chí Minh.
Số ĐKXB: 3239-2024/CXBIPH/05-107/TG
Mã ISBN: 978-604-4990-28-6
QĐXB: 533/QĐ-NXBTG ngày 12 tháng 9 năm 2024
In xong và nộp lưu chiểu quý III năm 2024

www.ingramcontent.com/pod-product-compliance
Lightning Source LLC
Chambersburg PA
CBHW050529240926
51846CB00003B/748
* 9 7 8 6 0 4 4 9 9 0 2 8 6 *